CONTENT

INTRODUCTION

I want to share my unedited truth about living with eating disorders.

The proceeds from this book will fund my endeavour to spread awareness and help people through their own struggles.

The following pages will lead you through my journey of mental health illness, including depression, anxiety, anorexia, bulimia and alcoholism.

I want to inspire people through sharing my recovery and give hope to those suffering, recovering or caring for someone affected by an eating disorder. I never thought I would be where I am today: healthy, happy, and the most confident I have ever been in my life. It has taken me a long time to get here and it is only now that I can look back and truly reflect on and see how far I have come. I feel like a completely new person, because I am finally free of my eating disorders. Freedom is the best gift you can ever give yourself and with recovery you can do that, and it is truly incredible.

I would like to thank everyone who has supported me on my journey, particularly my family and friends. Without your unconditional love, compassion and understanding, I would never have made it to where I am right now, or had the courage to share my experience in order to help others.

To everyone who supported my first book 'Raw, the diary of an anorexic', I am extremely grateful. It means a lot that you took the time to read my words and made an effort to understand a mental health issue that is becoming increasingly common. I have taken on board the constructive criticism and hope that this second edition will do it justice, with more pages dedicated to the all important recovery process.

To anyone reading this now, I hope you can gain a true and unsparing insight to the dark world of disordered eating and learn about the world of an illness you perhaps never knew existed.

Chapter 1
WHERE IT MIGHT HAVE STARTED

In September 2009, my parents drove me up to Newcastle to move into my flat for University. I was terrified, anxious and extremely nervous. I vowed to myself that I would only stay for a couple of weeks, before returning home to resume my life as normal. I ended up staying for two and a half years and cannot begin to describe how amazing my experience was. I loved every second of it and created some of the greatest memories of my life during that time.

Our six bedroom flat (located right opposite the bars in Jesmond) became the venue for pre-drinks, the 'go to' place for friends and friends of friends and friends of their friends. We spent a lot of our time going out, getting drunk, staying up all night and sleeping off our hangovers. Washing up became a rare activity and with all the partying and comings and goings, quite quickly the house became a complete mess. The mess turned to dirt and the dirt turned to filth. It got to a point where it would have actually been impossible to clean and I am quite surprised we didn't all get ill.

Living in this kind of environment was new, fun and exciting, however probably quite disruptive and unsettling. I think the chaos around me affected me in ways that I didn't realise at the time... I became great friends with a big group of people, all amazing, but I think I got lost in a world that was alien to me.

I remember this entire year of my life so fondly and think about it often. The wonderful friendships I formed, the excitement, the independence, crazy nights out, chaos, sleepless nights, impulsive decisions, drinking games, a whole new lifestyle and world of fun opening up before my eyes. I deeply miss lots of the people from that time and the precious moments that are embedded in my mind, which are some of the funnest, best and happiest memories of my life, before I lost it all. Perhaps my memories of that year are so important to me because I was free; I felt free, truly happy, and that's the last time I felt like that for a long time. I feel like it all happened too fast, and on so many occasions I have wished and longed to be magically transported back to that year, that amazing time I will always treasure.

Since day one of University, I was forever thinking there was something wrong with me. I was a self-confessed symptom-google-er and was always going to the Doctor to see if there was something wrong with me. ADD, ADHD, M.E and CFS were just a few of the many things I was convinced I had. I developed the name of a hypochondriac from all my flatmates, which was a funny joke, however it made me feel like people didn't take me seriously and that no one was actually listening to me, thus making me worry about something being wrong even more. What if something did actually happen, and then no one would believe me? I felt like the boy who cried wolf and didn't really appreciate my new nickname..

So maybe this is where it all began; after giving up chocolate for lent for the first time ever in Easter of 2010, I was so proud of myself to have proved everyone who thought I couldn't do it, wrong! It was extremely satisfying and was the thing that really showed me I could give up anything, should I put my mind to it... and I could lose weight, if I treated life like lent. On Easter Sunday my brother and I ate nothing but chocolate... chocolate for breakfast, lunch and dinner, and everything in between. We felt so sick from all the dairy and in turn, decided it would be a good idea to eliminate dairy foods for a year as some kind of detox or challenge, essentially becoming Vegan (both already vegetarian since the age of thirteen).

This new idea was a challenge, but after completing the chocolate challenge, I knew that I could do it, so I did. I took it very seriously and overnight, gave up all dairy products, thus changing my already vegetarian and gluten-free diet drastically. I loved becoming Vegan because I knew that I could do it if I put my mind to it. It was 'healthier' (my parents disagreed at the time), I felt powerful, I was developing a greater knowledge of foods, what they contained, what to avoid and what I could eat. It gave me a sense of control over myself, but what I liked the most, was the identity it gave me. How many Vegans do you know? Not many I am sure. Well, I wanted to be one of those 'not many'. It made me individual and rare, maybe special. (I wrote this sentence around six years ago when not many people had heard of Veganism and the only specifically Vegan product available at the supermarket was the first Alpro Soya milk, which Starbucks didn't even use then - how times have changed!)

Over this year I began to lose weight gradually, purely due to the dietary change. I ate a lot less as there was suddenly hardly anything I was able to eat. Most meals were either soup or tofu salad. I really liked this and it made me even more strict with what I was going to put inside my body. I had always felt like the fat one in my family. My mum and sister are both slender and my dad and brother, men... I always felt like the in-between one, the chunky one, the pig. Finally I was starting to feel a little lighter, a little more in control of my body with the help of this magical new way of eating.

Skipping forward to the summer of that year, I began to notice some changes down below... I ignored it at first, as I was too embarrassed to tell anyone. Weeks passed and the symptoms were only becoming worse, but I was still too afraid to face up to what was happening. When I moved home for summer, I guessed what was wrong; I guessed I must have caught an STI from one drunken mistake at Uni. I felt humiliated and sick with shame. How could this have happened to me when I know so many people who sleep with different people all the time and I never do! Why had they never had this? Why me? I couldn't get my head around how unlucky I must be.

Eventually, as the symptoms worsened I booked an appointment at the local clinic to go and get checked out. I couldn't tell my Mum, so I had to ask for a lift to the station to go 'shopping' for the day. No questions were asked and I went along to the hospital by myself, where I was diagnosed with genital warts. The humiliation and self disgust I felt when hearing those words said out loud was unbearable. Until years later, I was unable to say that hideous phrase myself. I was told I would need a weekly freezing treatment in order to get rid of them, which terrified me. How embarrassing! Would it be painful? How was I going to be able to lie every single week in order to get there?

At night I would lie beneath my covers crying for hours over what was happening to me, googling everything about my infection. I hated myself and I hated my disgusting body for contracting this hideous thing. The severe symptoms I had were not only very painful, but extremely unsightly, which further fuelled my disgust towards myself. I developed a deep anger towards my own body for letting me down and allowing this infection to be transmitted. My appetite was genuinely shrinking due to the deep depression this was all causing me, so I was eating a lot less but not even intentionally; I just didn't feel like it. Looking back now I think my loss of appetite may have gradually become a form of self-punishment. I didn't feel like I deserved food after what had happened and I wanted to teach my stupid body a lesson. This was still all very subconscious.

Every time I went for an appointment, they allocated a different nurse to do the freezing treatment. I felt so ashamed and embarrassed that every nurse in that hospital had seen my ugly private parts. I remember screaming in pain for them to stop during the treatment on numerous occasions as it was excruciatingly painful. It wasn't uncommon that I would faint during the treatment, due to the sheer pain. The warts were not going at all and by this point, there were loads. I felt hideous, inside and out, and it was all I could think about.

Eventually I confided in a good friend and she was the only person I told for a long time. She would drive me to my appointments and be there to comfort me after. Sometimes walking was agony and I had to stagger into the house after treatment trying not to let my family see my pain. It was an awful time for me and my unknown depression was silently growing, rapidly.

At the end of that long summer, I told my Mum the truth. She was amazing and only said that she felt sad for me, not disappointed in me (which didn't actually matter because I was disappointed in myself). She offered to drive me to all of my appointments, though I never let her come in.

Because of the STD, I needed to have a smear test early. My results showed I had abnormal cells (CIN1), which meant I would have to have this screening every six months, as well as a biopsy. I am the most squeamish person I know and these appointments haunted me. Again I fainted several times due to the pain. I remember lying on the hospital bed, tears streaming down my face, legs shaking and trembling as I squeezed the nurses hand. The CIN1 became CIN2 and for a few years I had to endure this procedure frequently, which was horrendous.

I decided that I may have depression and I could not cope. My Uni work that I was supposed to be doing over the summer was building up, as I had been so preoccupied with what was going on. I had left everything else to the last minute. My Mum arranged for me to see a private CBT counsellor for a few weeks, before I returned to Uni. For me this was solely for my depression, but for my mum it was also because I wasn't eating enough (in her opinion). I was also prescribed Citalopram (antidepressant), which seemed to help me and I felt a little better in myself.

I made myself sick for the first time ever that summer. It was a warm day and my driving test was at 1 o'clock. At twelve I ate a large bowl of butternut squash soup, AND a salad. I panicked about the amount of food and before I knew what I was doing I ran into the bathroom and emptied the contents of my stomach into the toilet. Orange mess splattered up the walls and my eyes were bloodshot and streaming with tears. I cleaned up the mess just in time for when my driving instructor arrived. I felt weak yet full of adrenaline, but only passed my driving test by one point. Up until that moment I had never even considered making myself sick and it was not something I did again in a hurry. I felt dizzy, confused and horrible.

I went to a festival at the end of that summer and actually had a great time, though I didn't eat much. I bumped into some friends from Uni and one remarked, "Hey skinny!'... Immediately I asked, 'What do you mean?' He just laughed and said that I had got skinny. This comment shocked me, but actually made me feel good about my body for the first time in a long time. I smiled inside as I let those all important words echo in my head. Now that I had been called 'skinny', I knew I had to keep up this accidental loss of appetite, this weight loss.

Upon my return to University in September I stopped seeing the therapist and changed hospitals to the one in Newcastle, where I now had to lie to all my friends about where I was disappearing off to during classes. There, they could see that the freezing treatment wasn't working with me at all and that it was totally pointless. They prescribed me a cream which they don't tend to give out as it is more expensive for the NHS. I tried it, and oh my god IT ACTUALLY WORKED. Very slowly my symptoms began to clear up and it was the best feeling in the world.

I started going out with someone I had liked for most of first year and he become my boyfriend. My second year of University was looking more promising than everything that had happened over the summer and I thought that maybe from now on, things would go well. My diet remained the same because although things were looking up, the habits I had created already had a firm place in my routine and I didn't even consider changing them back or ending the subconscious punishment.

I moved into my new flat with four boys. Some therapists have highlighted this living situation (of being the only girl) as a potential reason for my descent into

Eating Disorders. Although I loved living with them, never felt excluded and had great friendships with all of my flatmates, I admit I did find it increasingly difficult to find opportunities to eat in the house. Like in the previous flat, people were constantly coming in and out. Because the living room and kitchen were joined, I started feeling really embarrassed when making food in front of an audience of ten boys watching the television. I'm sure nobody would have even noticed, but in my head I felt as though people were watching me and would think that I was greedy. I didn't want to eat when no ones else was eating, so I didn't. I became extremely self-conscious.

I started eating in secret, a sandwich on the metro every now and then, a packet of crisps (or two) shovelled down my throat when no one was around. In the evenings when everyone would order takeaways, I would create a strange concoction of boiled rice in chocolate soya milk and drink sugary black coffee by the gallon. I stopped spending money on food as I decided I would rather buy nice clothes for when I finally liked my body... so I just used everyone else's rice from the cupboards.

My lunches at University became more and more estranged... I was eating from cans and jars now; nothing proper, nothing prepared, nothing cooked.

This bizarre diet that I seemed to be developing didn't come out of nowhere. It was a combination of my desire to lose weight, which had been there for years (I had just never stuck to diets or succeeded in my weight loss), the depression I was silently suffering and the self inflicted pressure and stress I heaped upon myself to be skinny, to live up to the identity I had created for myself. Again this was all very much subconscious and at the time I didn't see anything wrong with eating a can of sweet corn and a whole red pepper for lunch; it was cheap, vegan and convenient. I ignored the staring in the library and continued to eat from my can.

I feel like I spent that year trying to present myself as the cool, laid back, chilled out person I had tried to be in first year. The truth is: underneath everything, I was not cool; I was stressed, uptight, frantic, and struggling with depression and anxiety. I tried to give off the impression that I was floating along without a care in the world, when in reality, I was a tangled mess of emotions which I chose to ignore.

Just before the Christmas holidays, I was due to fly to Geneva to meet my dad and brother for a weekend of skiing. The evening before the flight, I was in a state of utter panic. I had an assignment due the next day, which I hadn't even started. I was panicking, very stressed and worked up. Before I even realised what I was doing, I found myself running to the corner shop in the snow, purchasing a large bag of doritos, and shovelling them down my throat behind the locked door of my bedroom. I then proceeded to the bathroom and puked every last orange dorito up. I washed my face and hands and locked myself back in my room to cry. My flatmates were amazing to me that night I remember; they calmed me down and helped me out. Nobody knew the true reason for the state I was in and even though I needed their comfort, I felt completely alone, isolated from the world around me, like no one could or would really understand anyway.

I completed my work at 4am and handed it in at 9. I then packed my bags and headed to the airport where I purchased a roasted vegetable wrap from Boots, ate it, and regretted it. Once in Geneva we drove up the mountain to our little hotel. At dinner I ordered a Salad minus the bread, then pretended to feel ill once we got back to our hotel room. I locked myself in our shared bathroom (my brother and dad just on the other side of the door) and made myself sick. They had no reason at all to be suspicious, as I had just told them I was feeling ill.

The skiing was amazing. I feel most free when I am flying down a mountain with fresh icy air soaring across my face. Even the sound of the snow under my skis excites me, I love everything about it. I had a great time with my dad and brother for the rest of the trip, mostly because I was able to momentarily escape the overwhelming thoughts I'd been having, whilst focussing on flying down a mountain.

We returned home for Christmas and I can't remember much about it, except desperately wanting to get back to University so that I could continue my eating plan without everyone's prying eyes. Christmas used to excite me, but I found that with it being such a food focussed holiday, I no longer had any interest. My Dad's Christmas present to my Mum was a family holiday to Cuba in the coming Easter Holidays. I was full of excitement, then fear - how the fuck was I going to wear a bikini next to my Mum and Sister? I decided I had to do something, something drastic..

Chapter 2
TU COLA DIETICA

2011

I returned to University for the spring term with every intention of getting back on top of things, back to my diet and to losing weight. I had been planning for a while what changes would need to be made and remember I was horrified to receive an extremely worried phone call from my mum, who had read a notebook I had left at home outlining these plans. She read out, "'Lunch - six raisins'. I hope you are joking". I assured her that of course I was joking after screaming at her for reading my private notes. I felt sick when I hung up, terrified she wouldn't believe me and would worry or interfere with my new lifestyle that I was carefully putting into place.

I announced to my two best friends on my course that I was going on a diet, to which they responded, "you have lost weight already, you don't need to lose any more", but of course I didn't believe them.

I continued on my weight loss mission by taking Veganism to the next level. My logic behind this was: if I could lose weight by following a Vegan diet, I could definitely lose even more weight if I became a Raw Vegan. I eliminated all hot and cooked foods overnight, including rice and my beloved Starbucks drinks. This easily ruled out most possibilities of eating out, as how many restaurants make Raw Vegan food? None. (Again, I wrote this sentence five years ago, a lot has changed since then, but at that point in time there were no Raw Vegan restaurants and barely any Vegan or Gluten-free options available anyway).

During this time I focused on my boyfriend, my coursework and my image. I spent much of my time in the library pretending to work (as I had no concentration span left) and avoided going home at all costs. My brain was noticeably slowing down and my energy levels dropping; instead of realising or accepting that this was due to my new eating restrictions, I chose to ignore it and fight against it. I knew I was nowhere near what I was aiming for, so continued to push myself despite these changes. Sugar-free Red Bull fuelled me through until the evenings, when I might have popped home for a quick can of sweetcorn and a black coffee, before heading straight back to the library. I was noticeably losing more weight and I liked it, it felt good. People's comments about my weight only added fuel to the fire, as the more people that mentioned my weight loss, the more it pushed me to lose more. It felt good that people were noticing me, noticing my achievement.

When it was time to sleep I would lock my bedroom door and dance in silence to burn the calories from the sweetcorn and whatever else I had put in my body that day. If anyone had seen me they'd have thought I was mental, which in a way, I guess I was. I would dance out every bit of energy I had before collapsing on my bed to sleep until the next morning, when it would all begin again. Apart from that, I didn't actually include any exercise in my strict regime at all. I tried running for a while but feared it was causing my legs to actually get bigger due to muscle gain, which wasn't what I wanted. So I stopped and didn't think to exercise again.

It was the Easter holidays... On the airplane to Cuba I refused the breakfast and picked at rice for lunch. The food in Cuba is pretty limited, most meals consisting of the staples - chicken, rice, beans, plantain and minimal salad, so I knew that by being Vegan, I wasn't going to have to try too hard to avoid food, as my options were limited already. This was great as it meant fewer excuses would need to be invented to get my family off my back.

For breakfast on day one I had fruit, oats and soya milk. By day two this became just fruit and soya milk and by day three - nada! From that point on I never ate breakfast again and that is the rule I made for myself that took me the longest to break.

I hunted down 'Tu Cola Dietica' (diet coke in Cuba) like my life depended on it and avoided any other sugary drinks like the plague.

I can remember one night so vividly. We were staying in a local lady's home in a rural town called Vinales. She prepared us an evening meal and I can't even actually remember what it was that I ate, but I felt like it was the end of the world. My whole family decided to walk up the road to watch some local music in a bar and I pretended to feel unwell and stayed in the house. I locked myself in my parents tiny bedroom (as it was a little bigger than my own) and spent the evening pacing up and down and up and down the few meters of space inside, trying to take as many steps as possible in the short amount of time I had alone. I jogged on the spot and did star-jumps in a desperate attempt to redeem myself from my sin of eating too much. I couldn't gain weight now, I had been doing so well..

Though I thought nothing of it at the time, I was sick several times during that holiday. We were on an idyllic little island called Cayo Levisa, staying in lovely wooden cabins on the beach with white sand and the crystal clear ocean surrounding us. The island was so tiny you could walk around it within an hour. One evening we had cocktails and supper in the restaurant on the beach while watching the sun go down. I felt like I had eaten too much (yet again). Rather than sit back, relax and enjoy the wonderful company and beautiful scenery, I had an overwhelming urge, a need to get rid of all the food. This need took over me and before I knew it, I found myself sprinting back to the cabin along the stunning beach, sticking my head down the toilet and making myself sick for a good ten minutes. I washed out my burning mouth, cleaned myself up and went back to the dinner table, smiling like nothing had happened. Everything was fine, just a little bit of sick, no big deal right?

I won't go into this holiday in too much detail as I don't wish to taint the incredible memories I do have of it. My family are so special to me and apart from the secret struggles I had during that holiday, I had an amazing time.

When we returned home two weeks later, I had noticeably dropped more weight. I also had hideous orangey-yellow hair. I'd always wanted to try being blonde and because it was cheaper in Cuba, I made the stupid decision to do it there. A big mistake - I looked like Vivienne Westwood gone wrong and was stuck with it for the rest of the holiday. My little cousin announced to me hours after the change, "you look really ugly with blonde hair". I cried in my room. I KNEW he was about ten years old at the time and obviously didn't mean or understand what he had said, but I truly believed him and let this get inside my orange head.

The following term of university is somewhat of a blur. I downed sugar free drinks in the library, smoked like a chimney (both cigarettes and weed), spent a lot of time at my boyfriend's house in Sunderland and ate even more abnormally than before. Several of my housemates noticed and made remarks like: "Lyds you need to eat more, you're disappearing". Of course these kinds of comments didn't make me think 'oh shit, you're right'; sadly they had the opposite effect. I took them as compliments and used them to push myself even further into my behaviours.

Chapter 3
FOOD RAGE

University all done for the second year, it was time for a girls holiday to Zante with some friends from back home. I was a fair bit thinner by this point, my parents were starting to get quite worried, as were my friends on the holiday. I managed to get Laxido (a soluble laxative) prescribed to me by my GP. I drank the sachets all the time throughout the day. My friends commented but I assured them that they were prescribed for medical reasons and they did not need to worry.

The main thing that sticks in my mind about this holiday was the pain of lying on a plastic sun lounger by the pool, which is what I did all day. Even though I layered several towels over the sun bed and brought the pillows down from my room, I could still feel my tailbone and spine pressing into the hard plastic underneath; it was agony. The only thing I questioned about this scenario was how other people could manage to lie on them and not be in pain... It didn't cross my mind that perhaps I was too thin, because I still felt ashamed of my body in a bikini, like I was bulging out of it, even if I wasn't.

My diet suffered further in Zante, cigarettes and diet coke being my staples. I was feeling quite low and depressed and stressing a lot about gaining weight on holiday. On our final night I can remember standing in front of a long mirror in my underwear and gasping at how much weight I had gained (I had in fact lost weight). I panicked to my friends about the invisible weight gain which I could see so clearly and even though they reassured me it wasn't true, I felt frantic. I did some exercises in the bathroom in the middle of the night in an attempt to redeem myself.

I returned home thinner than I had been one week previous. By now it was blatantly obvious to everyone (except me) that I was losing control.

My boyfriend and I had arranged to spend a weekend together in York when I got back and we had an amazing time. I do however remember on the first evening, we had to go in and out of about six different restaurants before we were able to find somewhere that I would agree to eat. Lunch the following day was a similar situation... He ate anything so it was really easy for him to grab something as we were walking around. I had to settle for a measly bowl of tomato soup in the M&S cafe. I was really starving after the whole weekend of drinking alcohol but not eating much at all and began to get really angry that I couldn't find anything that would be OK for me to eat (there were plenty of things but something inside me always had a reason why I couldn't, something just said no on my behalf and there was no arguing). This is what I describe as my 'food rage'. I'd describe it like this: imagine your favourite food in the entire world and you've been promised it all day. You know you are going to get it at exactly 6pm and you are counting down the hours. It is all planned and is definitely going to happen, so you spend the lead up to that moment restricting or having nothing, because you know that you are going to allow yourself that one moment of pleasure in the day. Come 6pm, it isn't there, it's not available or it doesn't happen for whatever reason. The disappointment is like a stab in the heart and a lump of anger and sadness forms in your throat. You feel empty, let down, pissed off, then furious. The sheer disappointment morphs into feelings of pure rage. Slowly you begin to use this rage as some kind of sign, some kind of sign from the universe that you didn't deserve what you were waiting for anyway, because you are too fat and shouldn't be allowed to eat. My mind would tell me this over and over and I would begin to believe it until I felt content with the deprivation, even grateful for it, like it was necessary and something was helping me stick to my plan. I allowed myself nothing as I needed to listen to the lesson I was being taught. I would still feel bitter but deep down, through the disappointment and upset, I would decide that it was for the best.

Food rage happened to me on so many occasions. Storming out of restaurants feeling so venomous and heartbroken when they had taken the only dish I would eat, off the menu (yes Wagamama, that's you). Screaming at my Mum because she forgot to buy something at the supermarket which I had decided was ok for me to eat, or because she made me food that I didn't want. "I DON'T WANT YOUR FOOD, I WANT MY FOOD. STOP MESSING UP MY PLANS!" Chucking cereal bowls across the room if someone dared to make a comment about what I was eating.

The summer at home continued with many arguments between me and my Mum, predominantly about food. I was restricting more and more and constantly defending my 'healthy lifestyle' to my family. I received many a lecture about the dangers of not eating enough and the damage I was doing to myself by eliminating so many different food groups. I could kind of see where they were coming from and I was admittedly slightly worried myself. I spent several evenings huddled under my duvet researching symptoms of Anorexia, wondering if maybe I had it. Funny thing is I had never really understood how anyone could have such an illness. I had always been a great lover of food and failed on so many diets. I definitely never ever thought that I, of all people, could develop that illness. The weakness, the chronic fatigue, the depression and the obsession with diet all rang very faint alarm bells in my head, but I never truly believed there was anything wrong with me, I mean, I wasn't even thin so it was impossible.

A close family friend offered me the opportunity to house-sit whilst they were on holiday in August. I jumped at the chance of escaping my parents prying eyes and irritating, controlling comments for a week. I needed some time to myself, away from the people who were doing their best to ruin my great progress. During my stay at their house I was to walk their three springer spaniels twice a day. 'PERFECT', I thought; exercise as well as the opportunity to control my diet even more. My Mum sent me to their house with a big hamper of my 'safe foods', which mostly all went straight in the bin as soon as she left; my list was getting smaller and smaller. There was no internet and no signal, meaning there was no hassle from anyone. It got pretty lonely as there wasn't much else to do apart from walk and think about food. I was only sick once or twice and restricted brilliantly. This is the point when I actually began to feel like I didn't even really want food anymore, I didn't need it. Craving it was more tiring than just accepting the fact that I wasn't allowed it and because I was starting to feel a little weak at times, I just didn't have the energy to waste.

One evening I had friends round to the house to stay the night with me. We drank lots of wine and I gave them the chocolates I had been given for looking after the dogs. They left quite early the next morning and I fell back asleep on a duvet on the floor. My Dad had come to the house to check up on me, saw me through the window asleep looking very weak and ill and voiced his concerns. He told me that I looked sick and needed to stop being Vegan or start eating more as I was really damaging myself and it was clear to see. Of course I told him that he was being absolutely ridiculous and that I was just hungover.

The summer is a pretty misty memory from then on. My boyfriend came to stay several times and we drank loads of Pimms, visited Camden and went to pubs. I saw my friends and relaxed but continued to restrict more and more and argued with my parents.

Chapter 4
PARISIAN DREAMS

By the end of that summer I had started counselling again. My mum was so worried that she had contacted my old CBT therapist and voiced her concerns about my ever decreasing weight and diet. Furious at first, I gave into her begging and agreed to go and see him (mainly to get her off my back). I insisted I was fine to both my therapist and my mum. I nodded and listened attentively whenever diet or food intake was brought up and then calmly disagreed with everyone else's views, insisting that I was fine and that everyone was just trying to control me. I wasn't fine though, my periods had stopped, I was noticeably very thin and fail, tired all the time, weak and angry. In this state of mind all I could think about was getting back to University, away from my family so I could get on with living my chosen lifestyle, a lifestyle of deprivation. I wanted to continue what I finally found out I was actually good at - losing weight!

I don't remember this at all, perhaps because my illness blocked it out, perhaps due to memory loss from a starvation diet, but my Mum told me recently that they tried to stop me from going back to University for my third year, in fact they begged me not to go back. They asked me to stand on the scales and show them my weight as I was in complete denial about how much I'd lost. I went mental at the idea, refusing, screaming and shouting at them for trying to ruin and control my life. There was nothing they could do, except for hope and pray that I would start to realise what was happening and turn things around. But I was already too far gone for that to be possible. The illness already had me in it's evil grips without me even realising it; there was no going back now.

In contrast to my living situation in second year of University, I moved into a big, clean house with six sensible girls. One of the six, Susie, had been my best friend since first year; we had been put into our first flat together by chance and formed a close friendship quickly. By the end of first year we did everything together; I even moved into her room and had a blow up bed on the floor so I could share her heater in the cold winter months!

The other five girls in the house were more Susie's friends than they were mine. Two of them had lived in the same building as me in first year, but in a different flat and the other two were from Susie's course. I had met them all lots of times on nights out and from visiting their previous house. They had all lived together in second year and invited me to move in with them. I leapt at the opportunity as although I had lots of fun with the boys, I recognised that I needed a more stable environment to live in, in order to concentrate on my final year of studying, and my diet.

I never felt particularly close to any of the girls I lived with, most likely because I was retreating further and further into myself. I became completely absorbed in my own routine and lifestyle, not having time for other people and taking no notice of what was going on around me. I also didn't have a huge amount in common with them as I had been used to living in a very different environment for the past two years.

Everything went fine at the start of the year (fine in the sense of the living situation). We all got along, I got stuck in to my Uni work, visited the boys in their house, paid visits to my boyfriend in Sheffield and felt generally on top of things. People of course commented on how much weight I had lost since they had seen me before summer, many looked pretty shocked when they saw me, but for me, this was just the complement of all complements! The hard work I had been putting in for so long was paying off. Finally, after years of trying to rid myself of those hideous squidgy muffin tops that (very slightly) spilled over my leggings, they had disappeared.

From this time on, there are very few pictures of me at Uni... I probably didn't want to be in any because I felt too fat, but my friends probably didn't want me in any because

I looked so thin. The girls often went on nights out and always invited me along. I rarely went with them because I didn't want to get all dressed up, I didn't like myself. I also got extremely tired very quickly and knew how exhausted I would be having such a late night. Knowing how cold I would get being outside in a dress, was another big reason. I also couldn't handle much drink anymore due to my weight and I didn't want those extra calories anyway.

I spent my time in University, away from people as much as I could. I developed a wonderful routine which seemed to fall into place with such ease. My life ran like clockwork. Over time, without me noticing, I was no longer dictating this routine, it had become so strict that it was dictating and controlling me. On my days of study I would allow myself two coffees in the morning. I would wake up super early, say six o'clock, run downstairs, bitterly cold, to refill my hot bottle and make a coffee. I would then return to my room and put on an episode of Supersize Vs Superskinny. As I watched the obese person's diet be compared to the skinny person's diet, I sipped on my coffee, smoked out the window, and smothered my gaunt, grey face in makeup. I was often late to Uni as I got so absorbed analysing the two polar opposite diets, wondering how I could be more like the super skinny, and less like the supersize. I was addicted to this television show and watched every episode of every season numerous times, as I had to watch it every single morning.

Make-up on face, I would scan my wardrobe, but always end up wearing the same damn thing... two pairs of tights, leggings, trousers, three thermal vests, a t-shirt, jumper, hoodie or two and a coat or two. It was ridiculous: it took ages to get dressed and it made me double the size, but I was so, so damn cold.

A month or so into the term, my dad arranged for me to go to Paris for a weekend with him. Paris is my favourite place and I was so excited. I flew out and met him there and vividly remember the worry in his eyes when he saw me at the airport. He looked at me like I was a total stranger, not his Lydia anymore. I have never seen him look that worried or scared - I felt really sad. We went to meet his friend for breakfast and I just ordered black coffees. My dad told me after, that while I was at the toilet his friend said to him, "She has Anorexia, doesn't she?" I was in complete shock and denial, I didn't know what they were talking about. When the weekend ended my dad and I sat on the steps of the Louvre in the baking hot sun. I remember how worried he looked, how sad he sounded and the look of fear in his eyes. He urged me to take more care of myself and begged me to eat more. I had an amazing time with him and I know he enjoyed spending time with me too, but something was different. The serious ending to the trip made me feel uneasy: guilty, like he wasn't pleased with me, but at the same time I knew that I couldn't start eating more just to please him, even though seeing him that sad and worried was one of the worst moments ever.

I got my flight back to Newcastle and returned to the house where all my housemates were sitting around the kitchen table. I hadn't eaten all day, so boiled some peas and lentils, then blended them together with water. I ate a small mug of the puree alone in my bedroom. Minutes later, I could not believe what I had just done. Thinking about the nutritional values of peas and lentils, I felt an overwhelming sense of guilt and disgust. I bolted to the bathroom, turned on the shower to disguise the noise, and forced myself to vomit the tiny amount of food. I cleaned up the bathroom, wiped the guilt from my mouth and the tears from my eyes and crept back to my room. I didn't go back downstairs; I went to bed and struggled to sleep.

This time is one of the most difficult for me to write about, not only because it was an excruciatingly lonely and painful time, but also because my diet had become so poor that I was really struggling mentally. My cognitive ability had deteriorated to the point where I was living almost in a trance. I felt high most of the time - high on starvation. I remember well the very amazing feelings and the very horrendous feelings, but not much in-between.

On days where I had University, my food intake was literally only for the purpose of preventing my stomach from rumbling in lectures. I had a massive paranoia of being in quiet places as I couldn't bare the thought of my body expressing it's hunger out loud; I found it so embarrassing. I used the salad bar at our canteen and filled the 'size small' plastic box less and less each day, counting the number of kidney beans I added. I remember one of the dinner ladies at the till scanning my pathetic, almost empty box of leaves and politely saying, "You know you can fill these right up. Why don't you go and get some more love? It will be the same price." I declined the offer and paid for my leaves which took more than half an hour to eat. I would still go out drinking and stumble home off my head, as my body really couldn't cope with alcohol anymore. Between the lectures and going out in the evening, I would collapse on my bed and nap for a couple of hours, in a feeble attempt to warm myself up and summon some inner energy.

On the days that I had off studying, I would still be up at the crack of dawn, as staying asleep for long was becoming impossible.

I trusted no restaurants, cafes, or food cooked or even bought by anyone other than myself. They could definitely be trying to trick me into eating more than I needed, and all I wanted was what I absolutely needed - nothing else. I didn't know whether people had tampered with or contaminated things, and became extremely paranoid. I thought people could potentially be conspiring against me and my plan. I limited the amount of toothpaste I used to brush my teeth incase I absorbed the calories. I wouldn't take any medicine or supplements, and sometimes drank less water on purpose as I thought it made me heavier.

One evening before I was due to go out, I ate a few teaspoons from a can. I remember thinking: 'holy shit, why on earth did I just do that when I had a couple of teaspoons earlier in the day? I didn't NEED that!' To the toilet I ran and got rid of the food. By this point Susie approached me and asked me quietly if I was ok. She told me one of the other girls had heard someone being sick a couple of times in the bathroom and thought it may be me. Absolutely horrified, I of course denied it. I was outraged that they thought it was me (even though of course it was). I insisted I had no idea who it could be and off I went.

Chapter 5
TEARING INTO THE NIGHT, WATCHING YOU SLIP AWAY, DARK IN DREAMS

I will take a minute out of this chaotic passage to talk about how I actually felt at this time, rather than just stating what I ate and how people around me were reacting. I discovered that a housemate across the hall from me had electronic scales in her room. I had never owned scales before, as my mum never saw the need for them in the house. This machine fascinated me. When everyone was out of the house I found myself sneaking into her room more and more frequently to step on this incredible glass square. It started out as once or twice a week, purely out of curiosity. This quickly evolved into me darting in and out at every single opportunity to see what number it would read. Standing on those scales made me feel amazing, proud, strong, independent, worthless, not good enough, like a failure, yet determined, all at the same time. The excitement and thrill I got from doing this was incredible: adrenaline pumping through my veins as I breathed deeply, mentally preparing myself to step on. I became so quickly addicted to seeing the numbers drop. If my weight had not decreased or had gone up by even a quarter of a pound, I would burst into tears, try and be sick, do star jumps, and reconsult the scales literally half an hour later, praying it would show me what I needed to see.

I remember getting below a certain number, and feeling the most triumphant I've ever felt about anything in my life. Adrenalin surged through me as I stared at the magical number I couldn't believe I was seeing. I had never been so proud of myself and I truly felt high like nothing else had ever made me feel. I was excited, amazed, relieved and genuine tears of joy filled my eyes. The thing is, all this made me want to do, was see that number drop further. This didn't mean I could stop. It meant I could do it and I should do it more, because I was actually good at it. I wanted to achieve that same high over and over again because it was the best feeling in the world.

I persuaded my mum and dad to buy me a full length mirror when they came to visit. For obvious reasons, they were reluctant, but I needed it, otherwise how was I supposed to see what I was doing. I wanted to watch my progress physically as well as numerically.

During their visit, I shed a few layers of clothing, to make what was going on look a little less obvious. I didn't want them to know how painfully freezing I was because I knew they would say I wasn't eating enough. We visited an old town called Beamish and I was frozen to the bone, desperately trying to pretend I was of a normal temperature. They didn't believe me for a second and their worried glances and comments throughout the day were difficult to ignore.

They took me to dinner twice on their visit and both times went the same way: me picking at a pathetic, undressed side salad. I couldn't eat. These dinners were not part of my detailed plan and inside I was brimming with fear and anxiety, imagining the numbers on the scales increasing. The nervous glances from my frustrated parents and awkward silences through both meals made it clear that everyone knew what the situation was, that I was really sick and that I was only getting worse, except I, myself, didn't know.

Due to losing such an excessive amount of weight in such a short space of time, my immune system had become compromised. I developed a terrible case of flu and was bedridden for a week or so. I could barely speak or move and I remember wondering whether or not I was going to die, living off Beachams and not much else. At night whilst lying in my bed, weeping to Bon Iver, I would send a text message to my family, friends and boyfriend, telling them how much I loved them. They were unaware that I was sending these texts because I was genuinely petrified that I was not going to wake up if I fell asleep. My throat was raw, head aching, coughing phlegm and feeling weaker that I had ever felt in my life. After about a week, I dragged myself to the doctor who told me I had a chest infection and gave me antibiotics. I did not discuss my weight or diet.

It was on the 19th October 2011 that I received a letter from my Mum which cut through my heart like a knife. My stomach dropped, throat tightened and tears ran down my face as I read it. I had been completely emotionless and glassy eyed for some time up until this point.

The letter read:

'Dear Lydia,

From the moment you were born I loved you with all my heart, and that love has only deepened with time. You are beautiful, smart, funny, kind, loyal, caring... (and so many more good things). You have so much going for you: loyal friends who love you, a lovely boyfriend, a family who love you (you mean the world to all of us). You have a great living situation this year and you seem to be getting stuck into work in a more positive way than last year or the year before. It is lovely hearing you sound so positive and excited for the future: thinking of Paris, styling, travelling etc.

You were brave for seeking help for your feelings of depression in the summer, and while the positive effects of the treatment are clear to see, it will be natural to have ups and downs - everyone does, but keeping on with the counselling will as you know help you deal with negative thoughts.

I have written a hundred letters to you in my head when I can't sleep for worrying about you, and I thought that I would try to write some of my worries down because I can't store all this up in my head for much longer.

Although you seem to be feeling a bit happier, you are continuing to get thinner and thinner. Everyone can see that you have an eating disorder and that you need help to get better - except that you can't see it. It is not your fault and you probably can't help it - that is what this illness is like. If you can't see how frighteningly thin you have become, then think about how you feel. Cold? Tired? Aching body? Low in energy? Etc etc. Is this how you want to spend the rest of your life? You don't have to. This flu and its complications is not surprising. Your defences will not be able to fight off germs as your immune system has been compromised. You used to read a lot about illnesses that you thought you might have. Well now that you have this, I wonder if you have looked up any information about it. There are some useful websites e.g.
    B-eat

ABC anorexiabulimiacare
Supportline.org.uk/problems/anorexia

Effects of a starvation diet:
I think you already know some of the long term effects,
e.g.

- Body metabolises / eats its own muscle to stay alive
(this is happening to you now)

- Can lead to heart disease and even heart attack

- Osteoporosis / bone wasting disease - all the minerals
are leached out of your bones causing them to become
brittle and fragile and break easily. Also, you shrink, and I
can see that your posture has changed; you have become
hunched. If this is left to continue, your body will sadly
become more like that of a frail 90-year-old woman than a
young 20 year old.

- Loss of periods / fertility - if not corrected early
enough, you may never know the joy of creating a family
with someone you love. This would be so sad.

- Dry skin, pale yellow complexion, dry brittle hair,
which then starts to fall out, fine downy hair growing on
the face and body... the list goes on. If left untreated you
will get worse and worse until you are hospitalised. I don't
want that and I'm sure you don't either.

The thing is Lydia, that you can choose to continue along this path or to turn things around and to get better. I know it must seem a very hard step to take - to firstly admit that you have a problem, and then to say that you want to get better (to someone, anyone, DR?) There is lots of help there but you need to want it. You are a strong person and I hope and pray that you will have the courage to seek this help ASAP, and to take control in turning your life around for the better. It won't be easy (the hardest thing will be the first step), but you will have us all and your friends to support you. Everyone wants you to get better. The sooner professional treatment begins, the better the outcome.

Please please please, I beg you, (we all do), please want to get better.

I will always love you,

Mum xoxoxox'

After reading this letter I was speechless and numb. I hid my head under my covers and cried like I hadn't cried for a long time. It was the opening paragraph that hit me more than anything, as well as the line: 'Everyone can see that you have an eating disorder, and that you need to help better - except that you can't see it'. By this point I was no longer afraid of the damage I was causing myself. I knew all of the effects, long term and short term, but I was SURE I didn't have this disease. How could I? I wasn't even that thin! Everyone was just exaggerating and being very, very dramatic.

I am not going to lie, I have spent hours of my life on websites created by other anorexia sufferers; some being 'proana' / 'mia' (promoting anorexia and bulimia), some being pro-recovery (promoting recovery of eating disorders), some being a bit of both. I find it both astonishing and frightening how many proana / promia sites appear through search engines when looking up the disease. When attempting to research recovery, my page became subsequently swamped with websites promoting eating disorders, which in my vulnerable state, I (and I am sure many other people) ended up clicking on. Many of these websites glamorise the horrific disease, as well as offering 'tips' and 'advice' on how to enter the world of dangerously disordered eating. These websites are plastered with unrealistic images of celebrities, models and severely ill individuals to act as 'thinspiration', in order to encourage and motivate the delicate minds of those who are already victims of anorexia and those who are potential sufferers.

These websites are sick; they can suck you in, and I decided that these people were real anorexics and I wasn't. I justified this by considering several points carefully. Many of the websites mentioned intense exercise. I didn't exercise at all; I simply, physically couldn't. These girls were running miles a day on an empty stomach. I was so weak that I had to crawl up the stairs of my house; there was absolutely no way I would be able to go running, even if I tried! This meant I definitely was not anorexic, because if I was, I would be able to summon the strength and energy to exercise as well as diet, and that just wasn't an option due to my weakness.

None of these girls seemed to drink milk. I drank half a soya Starbucks most days and when I got almost halfway through the sugar-free drink I would power walk to the closest bin and automatically throw the rest away. There was no choice involved in that daily action, I wasn't even allowed to consider drinking more, it was robotic. I never questioned or argued when I reached halfway, I just did it. I knew I had to.

So my conclusion was this: yes, I had many of the side effects, constantly frozen to the bone and unable to warm up, I was quite thin now, with a hunched back (thanks Mum), inability to concentrate, extremely malnourished which in turn was making me feel very physically weak, constantly sleepy, skitzy, unable to sleep, all over the place, loss of periods and generally ill, BUT, I was not thin enough, nor did I exercise, and I still drank soya milk, so there was absolutely no way I was anorexic and even if I was, I clearly wasn't a very good one, or a real one!

I cannot remember the conversation I had with my mum about the letter she sent me. I am sure it would have been something along the lines of me reassuring her that I was absolutely fine, that I knew all the dangers, and that I promised I would eat more, even though it definitely wasn't necessary.

During this month my younger sister came to visit me in Newcastle. For my project, I was creating a Parisian magazine entitled 'Pascale'. I love my sister more than anything in the world and was so excited for her to come and visit. I was going to use her as a model for my photoshoot, 'Le jour de Pascale', while she was visiting me. I remember the shock on her face when she arrived. I tried to ignore it and we went along as normal. She was however noticeably much quieter and contained than I had ever seen her. She seemed on edge the entire visit and couldn't really bring herself to look at me properly. Because of this, I tried doubly hard to make her feel welcome. I baked her cakes and bought her a Waitrose breakfast and hot chocolate early in the morning. I wanted her to feel safe with me and for her to see how fine I was. I could tell however, that she did not feel safe with me, she felt scared of / for me. I cannot imagine what it must have been like for her to see me like that, looking like a walking skeleton, very, very sick, yet completely oblivious to it. It must have been an excruciatingly difficult few days for her and I still feel awful about it now. My dad told me later that after I had put her on a the train home and he collected her from the station, she got into the car and burst into tears. She told him that as soon as she had got on the train, she was holding back tears the entire journey home. She was terrified for me and shocked from seeing her big sister looking so unwell. I felt like I had let my little sister down, and it was devastating.

A letter she wrote to me some time later:

'Lydia,

I wanted to write you this letter as I find it hard to express how I feel in any other way.

I know you think you are ok and that we are all being ridiculous, but as far as I'm concerned and anyone else is, you are far from it. I know it's hard for you to see something is wrong.

I even remember lying to myself and pretending everything was ok and normal, but this all really hit me that time I came to visit you in Newcastle. You were getting changed and I just felt this huge lump in my throat as I had convinced myself everything was fine, but it was one of the worst moments ever. When I got on the train after saying goodbye I instantly started to cry but tried to force myself to hold it in. Then I got in the car when Dad picked me up from the station and burst into tears. The harsh realisation of it all was overwhelming.

I know that it is so hard for you to see me upset, so I try and stay strong for you but sometimes I find it hard to deal with. I also know that you can have the drive and goals so prominently one day, but then non-existent the next.

Anorexia has completely changed you and not of your own fault. I have lost the Lydia that I loved spending time with, fighting over clothes with. I am adamant for you to get better so we can do the things sisters should do. I want to be able to go clubbing with you in London, go to Thorpe Park, go skiing, ice skating, anything!

It is so difficult for you as you are constantly battling the voices in your head. Although you have reassured me not to be scared or worried, that is naturally impossible for me as your sister. There are so many possibilities of things that could happen, triggered by this disease and they are constantly on my mind.

By writing this letter I am not trying to blame you for any of this, or make you feel guilty... that is in fact the last thing I want to do. I just want you to understand better how I am feeling, as I find it difficult to express a lot of the time.

I love you so, so much that you don't understand, and I just don't want to lose any more of my sister than I already have. I hope this can inspire you to an extent and help you realise that I believe you are strong enough to get through this. I have always thought you are beautiful and 'ana' has only made you change, and not for the better.

I want my older sister back - to achieve that you have to to eat to function properly, and to do all the things we miss doing together.

All my love,

Your baby sister,

Paskey xoxoxoxoxo'

I went to see several doctors over the course of these months, none of whom took much notice of my weight even though I vaguely queried it. One elderly male doctor even prescribed me appetite-increasing pills as a solution (which of course went straight in the bin), and didn't even consider the possibility of an eating disorder. Subconsciously this disheartened me. It was like I had summoned the courage to almost ask for help and had been rejected. If four different doctors didn't think there was anything wrong with me, then there must not be. I assumed I was being pathetic, dramatic and continued on my dangerous path.

Early diagnosis of eating disorders is crucial. Look up any information about the disease, and the importance of this fact is emphasised greatly. It took me way too long to get officially diagnosed. Anorexia, when left untreated or unnoticed, only worsens over time as the disease manifests within the victim. Habits and compulsions develop, grow and strengthen, leaving the sufferer to become more and more absorbed in their illness. The gaps of escape and clarity become smaller, as the illness traps you in. If the issues are addressed early on or as the disorder is developing, chances of full recovery are increased significantly. The longer you leave the behaviours to become ingrained and routine, the more difficult they become to break away from and change.

Looking back, I am genuinely appalled at how long it took for a medical professional to realise what was wrong with me, especially when I was forever expressing my fears that something was not right and dropping blatant hints about my struggles with food. It took a ridiculous amount of time, appointments and doctors for me to get the diagnosis of Anorexia Nervosa, when it was clear to my family and others for some time, that I had it.

Until you hear those cutting words: 'Anorexia Nervosa', you continue to believe that there is absolutely nothing wrong. You don't want to believe that you have this shameful disease; you think you are well and just very controlled and great at losing weight. That is what I thought anyway. Never in a million years did I think I could have such a thing, and it's too easy to carry on keeping your fantasy world that you have created, if left alone with Anorexia.

It was not until late October / November that I went to see the doctor again. I actually only went to go on the contraceptive pill, but perhaps in the back of my mind I knew things were not right and I maybe wanted someone to notice. I saw a lovely lady doctor who immediately voiced her concerns about how emaciated I looked. After telling her I had lost my periods and found it very difficult to eat, she weighed me and asked me to come back and see her the following week. This went on for several weeks and each time I saw her, I had lost more weight. She became very concerned and referred me on to an eating disorders specialist, which I very reluctantly agreed to.

Chapter 6
TRANCING IN THE MOONLIGHT

Letter from my doctor:

'18 November 2011

To Whom It May Concern:

I have been seeing Lydia at H**** Medical Group since the beginning of October. For some time Lydia has struggled with anxiety and depression and has been restricting her diet in order to lose weight. In the last few weeks she has been seen and assessed by our Regional Eating Disorders Unit and has been diagnosed with Anorexia Nervosa. Lydia is undertaking a community based treatment program and her mum has moved up to Newcastle to support her with this. The Eating Disorders Consultant is doing this as a trial over the next couple of weeks but it may come to a point where Lydia has to be admitted to an in-patient bed on the Eating Disorder Unit in Newcastle.

Lydia is currently attending the Eating Disorders Unit twice a week to have blood, heart tracings and weight assessments. She is following a strict diet treatment plant.

Yours Sincerely

Dr * *******'

It was on my fifth or sixth appointment with this lovely doctor that she dropped the bombshell on me. She had been away on holiday with her family for a week, so by the time she got back I had lost yet more weight. She told me very calmly that she couldn't sleep on her holiday for worrying about me. She had two young daughters herself and it broke her heart seeing me in the place I was. She said she would want to be told if her daughter was going through such a time. It was for this reason and the immediate danger I was in, that she had no option but to breach my privacy and contact my parents. I had not confessed my diagnosis to my family and didn't really intend to, as I didn't really believe it myself, and didn't want to worry them, or let them know that they were right. The doctor had been urging me to explain to them what was going on, but I refused. Later that day I got a phone call from my distraught parents who were in the car doing the six hour drive up to to Newcastle already. I was petrified. I did not want them to come up and interfere. I was fine. I cried to the doctor for going behind my back, how dare she, these appointments are strictly confidential. I genuinely considered suing her. Her reply was that if an intervention did not take place soon, I was going to die.

This was the first and not the last time that I heard these terrifying words: "you are going to die". They did hit a nerve within me, but at the same time, I wasn't entirely sure that I even cared anymore. Maybe I wanted to die. I definitely wanted everyone to leave me alone and let me get on with my life.

Prior to this intervention, my flatmates were becoming increasingly worried. Understandably they didn't really know what to say or do. Perhaps they did encourage me to eat more, but I can't really remember them doing so. It must have been horrible for them to watch; I know it was. On frequent occasions one or more of them would disappear off for a weekend at home. I was completely oblivious to the fact that this was partly because they found it too upsetting and difficult to watch me self-destruct. I was dying before their eyes and they were scared.

I staggered round the house and crawled up the stairs like a spider. My pyjamas hung off my jutting hips and shoulder bones as I scuttled into the kitchen to fill my hot water bottle for the millionth time. I could see them staring at what was left of my emaciated body, but I was convinced I was finally starting to look thin and nice, and that they must all be so jealous. They would all be sitting round the kitchen table laughing, joking, eating and drinking and then I would breeze in and slice the atmosphere with my sharp bones. The room would always fall quiet, as if a ghost had entered and they could feel its presence.

Unbeknown to me, during the time of my flu, my housemates had in fact sent an email to my dad. To this day I do not know exactly what it said, as I have never seen it. It was along the lines of how sick I was and how they were afraid to look in my bedroom in case I was dead. Their parents had also phoned mine to tell them that they needed to come and help me. I was affecting all the people I was living with and making it very difficult for them to get on with their work and their fun, as they were constantly worrying about me.

Obviously my parents knew all of this; they knew it was serious and they wanted to come and rescue me. They had been worrying and pleading with me to get help for months. The fact that I was over eighteen years old however, posed the issue that technically there was literally nothing they could do except for encourage me to get help, which they did, but I ignored them.

Amazingly, I was still managing to drink alcohol and go on nights out occasionally. I was drinking at the boys' house before going on a big night out. One of my friends pushed me, very lightly, but this was enough for me to lose balance and be knocked over. I fell straight into the table, but was fine. My lack of balance and strength shocked both me and everyone in the room. I was wearing a lot of thick jumpers over my black dress that was now so big, there was room enough for at least two more of me in it. My boyfriend picked me up and swirled me around when we arrived. Later that night, he said, "you're too thin Lyds". I knew something was wrong as he could barely look at me. He told me I weighed nothing when he had picked me up earlier and that he was terrified. This was probably the first time that he had pointed out my weight to me so directly, and it really hit a nerve.

Another example of when things got really bad prior to my diagnosis, was when my boyfriend came to stay for a weekend. I was becoming more and more absorbed in my illness. I wasn't sure who I was anymore and found it difficult to find things to talk about. I was unsure what was real and what was a dream. I questioned everything and understood nothing. I had retreated so far into myself that by this point, I could barely hold a conversation at times. I remember we were drinking in Weatherspoons at lunchtime, and I was sitting there desperately trying to think of something interesting to say, but I was completely blank. What did I used to talk about and laugh at? Nothing was funny and I had no interest in anything. I could not understand what we used to laugh and joke about, so I sat there in silence. He was trying to make an effort but I really genuinely couldn't find anything to say. It was a strange feeling. I felt like I was not me at that point - I was locked tightly away, out of sight, silenced. I didn't know who I was. I had lots of days like this. Some days I would be slightly more myself again, but within moments the anorexia could consume me and I would become a completely different person. My boyfriend told me it was like the exorcist; my face, voice and state could change within seconds and I would suddenly be dead behind the eyes, no longer Lydia.

He asked me to get the metro with him to Sunderland to stay with him at his parents house. I had to force myself, as I was so weak. I could barely walk and hadn't eaten anything for some time. I remember genuinely wondering if I would survive the journey and make it to his house. I had basically stopped eating altogether now. I was barely sleeping, as I didn't want to close my eyes and drift off incase I died in my sleep. I would lie in bed terrified, listening to Bon Iver, knowing that my weak heart could stop beating at any moment, and I would be gone. I was also having the most horrendous nightmares every time I did sleep. Most of these consisted of me scoffing an entire roast dinner and waking up sweating and screaming in fear that I actually did it.

When I got to his house I crept to the sofa in the kitchen, scorched my paper-thin skin with a hot water bottle and lay there, lifelessly. I could barely move. I was sure I was definitely dying now. His parents looked so worried as they offered me food, which I declined. Not only was my body disappearing, my personality had died and my voice had become a whisper. Everything sounded too loud to me; why was everyone always shouting and moving so fast? I was hypersensitive to everything, particularly the cold and sounds.

I struggled to sleep that night, but I was too withered and zoned out to do anything, even talk. I lay on my side curled up in a ball staring blankly at the wall. My entire body ached all over and I knew this could be it. I got the metro back to Newcastle the following morning, alone. He wanted to stay and spend some time with his parents. Later that day when he came to see me, he told me that his parents had phoned mine and told them how deathly ill I looked, that something needed to be done, fast. Obviously I was quite annoyed that they had all been talking about me and had contacted my parents, but I was too weak and exhausted to react or show any emotion.

Chapter 7
MIRRORS AND MIST

I was in a group at university for a business module
with two of my close friends, another friend and someone I
didn't really know. We had to set up and manage our own
business, working together as a team. I didn't do anything.
They could see how sick I was and I would turn up to help
them on the projects, only to have to leave and go home
because I was so cold and weak. I was utterly useless to the
entire project and completely clueless as to how they could
concentrate on something so boring and complicated.

One night we went to sell our goods at a bar. I put on
my sparkly high heels, baggy leggings and a jumper. I felt
like I finally looked pretty amazing. I got drunk and had a
lovely evening. I had a conversation with one of my
lecturers who attended the night, and that conversation
inspired me so much. She told me it was great that I had
come out, but I needed to sort out what was going on. She
said she had wanted to bring vitamin drinks to our lessons
for me on several occasions, because if I wasn't going to
eat I could at least drink. We talked about ways in which I
could inspire myself through glamour, fashion and film.
She told me to watch old movies and escape through
reading and ideas. It was an amazing conversation and it lit
a light bulb in my head. I confided in her and explained

how I didn't really know who I was anymore. Our conversation hit the right nerve and I will remember it forever.

When I got in at 23:59 I wrote this note in my phone:

'The worst thing is having to think about it and talk about it all the time. Having fun, being creative, inspiring people and films and ideas take you away. Drawing, ink, outfits, glamour, ideas, aspirations are a saviour. Confidence. Influence and inspiration are key words. Nothing is safe but everything is amazing. Creativity and drive will save me. Excitement and networking and listening and hearing other people. Record everything I see that I like. A scrapbook of influence and inspiration. A blog of influence and inspiration.
Take me away.
Find my escape.
Escape is creativity. Creativity is escape.
I think too much.
Life is about exploring and discovering.'

From this point on I used my phone notes religiously to record my thoughts and feelings, as well as many crazy ideas and dreams that I had. I felt enlightened. I was now running on a weird mixture or adrenalin, starvation and nervous energy. Combined, these fuels made me feel alert, invincible, powerful and generally wired. I felt euphoric, as though I could achieve anything I wanted and that I had the power to defy nature and survive on nothing. I wasn't like any other person around me; I had some special force within, to stay completely in control of my body. To me, everyone else seemed so bland, so conforming to the ideas of society. They woke up, ate, got on with their day-to-day tasks. I was always awake, never ate and had a mind spilling with important epiphanies, a special knowledge and outlook on life that no one else could even imagine. I did not need anything, sometimes not even water. I did not need people telling me I was sick. How did I know THEY weren't all sick? I was above all these people, floating in clouds and sparkles, on edge constantly, a beautiful nervousness and buzzing feeling that I could not describe. I was completely high on starvation.

I now see and understand that the true reason I felt this way was because I had starved my brain to the point where my cognitive ability had become so compromised that I was confusing dying with feeling more alive than ever. In that state I really did see the world in a different way to everyone around me, as I described it above; through a blur of mist that made me dizzy.

My identity became my eating disorder, and my eating disorder was my identity. I looked in the mirror and finally could not believe how thin I had got. I gazed at my stick-like legs, ran my blue fingers over my protruding ribcage like a piano. My face was sunken, my cheekbones like daggers. The largest part of my body was my haunted eyes, which stared back at me in the mirror in a state of pure amazement and maybe triumph at what I had achieved. I bought a pair new jeans which dangled around my stick like legs and hung so loose around my waist and bottom, that I had to wear three pairs of tights and a pair of leggings under them just to keep them on. My hip bones poked out through my clothes, my stomach was concave and my elbows sharp as knives. My breasts were completely non-existent and even a child's bra sat inches away from my chest. My knickers didn't even fit, as I no longer had a bottom. They hung limply off me and resembled a loose nappy. Yes, to you this many all sound extremely unattractive, but I truly thought I finally looked ok, good even. I did not look real, I looked like some strange mystical creature and that is what I felt like.

In contrast though, I felt fearful. Fearful of death at times, but then when I was feeling euphoric I could not care a less. Such a mix of these powerfully contrasting emotions is almost impossible to describe unless you have been through this yourself. Even then though, I cannot say that other people felt the same. This mesmerizingly haunted world that I was living in was miles away from anyone else and everything else.

After University every day, I would not go home but instead would pace in the darkness of the bitterly cold winter evening to Fenwicks department store. I would wander round and round aimlessly for hours gazing at all the beautiful objects. I became unbelievably observant and thought everything was stunning. How had I not noticed all of these amazing things before? The home section was my favourite. I would look at everything gold and fantasise about being rich and having all these incredible items in my future luxury apartment. I was constantly thinking about other people and buying them things. I spent so much money getting people presents because I just wanted to make everyone else happy. I wanted to give everything and take nothing, to make other people happy because they deserved it and I didn't. I spent lots of time baking the most fattening chocolatey cakes and handing them out to friends, watching in delight as they consumed a 600 calorie slice. I was obsessed with baking, looking up recipes and reading menus. Providing other people with food yet never letting myself have any was so satisfying. This made me feel like I had the ultimate control, as well a purpose... I could make all these delightful desserts, resist them and watch other people revel in the taste and gain weight -haha.

I know this is a common symptom of Anorexia; perhaps I was controlling myself so strictly that I was unable to go any further with it, so controlling the calorie intake of those around me was a tool I used to make myself feel better, even lighter.

I listened to a song called 'Spiral', on repeat. The lyrics: 'nothing's really sane but everything's amazing', were constantly in my head. It was exactly how I felt about life... That line is the best description of the emotions that had consumed me.

I was walking everywhere now; forty minutes to Uni, forty minutes back. Up every flight of stairs I could find, the longest routes possible and round and round town, in and out of every shop. I must have walked around Eldon Square shopping centre hundreds of times within those few months. I had been told to stop walking so much and was supposed to get taxis everywhere as part of my treatment plan. My mum even bought me a leopard print wheelie suitcase to carry my books to university, as I was burning up too many calories carrying my huge bag around. I ignored both these suggestions and carried on doing what I thought I should.

The only way in which I was able to warm up my permanently icy body was by sitting in a bath full of boiling water, and I had to do this every night. Showers were out of the question as I just felt too cold. I would run the bath as deep as I could before the water began to get cold. I would absolutely dread taking my clothes off to get in. As I peeled away each layer, the pain of the cold would get more intense, until I was standing naked, bony and pale blue. I would lower myself carefully into the tub until my sharp tail bone clunked against the bottom. It was so painful to sit that I had to lie back, feeling each bone of my spine hit the hard surface as I did. Sometimes I would exhale all of the air out of my lungs and lie under the water, just to see what it might feel like to not be in the world anymore. I would imagine drowning and feel peace in my underwater escape from the world, and only bring myself back up when I had completely run out of oxygen. I would look down at my bony, purple knees that bulged out of my birds legs and examine my skeleton, as I shivered in the boiling water. I would stroke the layer of fur that was developing on my arms, and wonder whether I HAD taken things too far, whether I was too thin now; I felt a little scared sometimes. When clumps of my hair came out in my hands as I washed it, I experienced moments of clarity searing through the cracks of my disorder. These moments were ten times more terrifying than being blissfully ignorant to the fact that I was killing myself. These moments made me feel sick to my stomach as I would momentarily panic about what I was doing to myself. I blocked them out with all my might till the voice of reason (or unreason) chimed in quickly, reminding me how well I had done, how good I was looking, congratulating me for achieving 'skinny' and telling me I had to keep going, because there was no way out now anyway - I couldn't possibly turn back. The punishment for a slip up would be too painful. Getting out of the bath was the worst part. I would count down, leap out, and jump for my towel, shivering and feeling physically sick with that icy cold that never left me. I would dart to my bedroom down the hall and blast the hairdryer on the highest temperature over my transparent skin, in a desperate attempt to heat myself before diving under my covers to my ready prepared hot water bottle, burning my delicate skin.

Another thing I did a lot around this time was sit on benches. I would just walk around town completely dazed and sit on benches anywhere by myself and think of nothing. I was completely blank and glazed over, but horrendously lonely, cold and depressed at the same time. I remember sitting on a bench in town outside a church for several hours once and feeling nothing, until I felt one tear slide down my sad face, then another and another. I didn't move, I just sat there, blinking terrified tears but feeling powerless to them. I felt like I had nowhere to go, no one to talk to and nothing to say anyway. I ended up going into the church and sitting talking to myself, or maybe God. I had no idea what to do with myself. I was so sad.

After my diagnosis I was in complete denial. I was so detached from reality that I could not differentiate between dreams and real life events. I was referred to the Regional Eating Disorders Unit in Newcastle (REDS) and was 'given the chance' to attempt recovery as an outpatient, on the condition that my parents moved to Newcastle to support me. The mere idea of this, horrified and infuriated me. Newcastle was MY world, how dare it even be suggested that my parents trespass into my end of the country, into my separate life.

Though I fought against this barbaric suggestion, it soon became clear to me that my say was becoming increasingly limited. My mum and dad took it in turns to stay in hotels near my house. They said they would not have to see me all of the time, they would only be there to support me. This filled me with an overwhelming sense of guilt and sadness; picturing my mum or dad sitting alone in a small hotel room whilst I was trying to ignore the fact that they were there, but that's the way it was.

Both my parents came to my consultation with the head psychiatrist at REDS. She was a large, fearsome looking woman whom I immediately decided I hated. She led me through the in-patient unit alone, to assess me. On the way through, we passed several demented looking skeletons. I gasped at how thin and emaciated they looked (unaware that to others, I looked the same). As sick and twisted as it sounds, I felt jealous of them. I also felt embarrassed to be there. They must all be wondering who this fat girl is and why she is here - she doesn't have anorexia! Funnily enough, I have no doubt now that we were probably all thinking the same thing, eyes darting, analysing and comparing our bodies in a swift glance. Sizing up the 'competition'.

I was taken into a small room where I had to strip. She weighed me, checked my teeth for acid erosion - none, my knuckles for scars from sticking my fingers down my throat to purge - none, my nails for discolouring - none. My temperature and blood pressure were low, but I put this down to the bitter cold of the North of England and the fact that my mum had always had low blood pressure. She made me squat down to the floor and stand up again - which I used every morsel of strength in my body to do perfectly. They make you do this as the muscles in the legs correlate quite closely to that of your heart, therefore they can get some idea of how weak the organ has become.

I came out of this assessment laughing to myself and even more convinced that there was absolutely nothing wrong with me at all. "I passed every silly little test of hers with flying colours", I boasted to my parents. So what, I had got pretty thin; but thats all I had ever wanted, so why was everyone kicking up such a fuss.

To my horror I was assigned a dietician. She was a kind, quiet woman who I could tell in a second would be so easy to manipulate. She prescribed me Ensure calorie drinks which I flatly refused as they contained milk and I was Vegan. Together we wrote a diet plan instead and I was instructed to keep and accurate food diary (which I had loads of fun making up to the finest detail before each appointment).

I was sent to the supermarket to buy the foods that I had agreed to eat. I asked my flatmate to come with me as I was pretty scared. I almost had a panic attack in the cereal aisle due to what seemed like hundreds of colourful, evil boxes staring at me. Why were there so many, how on earth was I supposed to eat any of them when they all contained over 100 calories per serving, what even is a serving of cereal, look at all that sugar, oh my god, oh my god. I scanned the shelves for ages for the lowest calorie option of each agreed food. I was horrified and thought no way in hell was I ever eating ANY of this disgusting calorie-laden poison. I would get fat all over again and all my hard work would be ruined and for nothing.

I became a serial liar, purchasing all the said foods and pretending to do my best to eat them. In reality I was eating even less and every item was discarded portion by portion into the bin, carefully hidden beneath everyone else's rubbish. This was surprisingly easy to do, as my housemates never said anything and I convinced my parents that I was participating to my best ability, trying my absolute hardest to get better.

One evening I was sitting on the cold kitchen floor, tailbone jabbing into the tiles, smoking out the back door. I felt nothingness. I knew I was dying and it genuinely didn't phase me. I slumped against the wall as a housemate attempted to confide in me. I cannot remember the exact conversation, I just remember saying that I didn't really care anymore; I was giving up and wasn't going to fight. I wanted to die. She was horrified and cried and pleaded with me not to say such things. I looked at the floor blankly. I had run out of things to say, I had run out of energy, I had run out of life, and the desire to live.

I visited the hospital around three times a week for consultations, weigh-ins, heart monitoring, counselling and meetings with the dietician. My heartbeat was irregular. Because of my extremely low weight, the antidepressants I was on were causing my (ever-weakening) heart, issues. I was immediately taken off them and felt lower and lower. Every week I had needles stabbed into my collapsing veins. Though they bulged out of my toothpick arms, it was a frequent occurrence that no blood could be extracted. I had to sit there as they pulled the needle out and searched for a 'better vein' to steal my blood from. After this, I would be plastered up and sent for my ECG. Stripped to my underwear, I lay on a cold hospital bed, freezing. Wires were stuck all over my body and attached to a machine to monitor my heart. I found this all very boring, and the waiting around pissed me off so much. I didn't want to be wasting my life sitting in a hospital in the first place, but then to have to wait for all this shit to be done to me, the fucking cheek of it!

Chapter 8
NOTHING'S REALLY SANE BUT EVERYTHING'S AMAZING

It was my dads turn staying in Newcastle. I have always had an extremely strong connection with him; he is one of my best friends and my hero. He would never judge me for anything and I always believed I was his secret favourite. One evening after we went out for supper (I pretended I had already eaten and ordered a glass of wine instead), I felt so low after he had dropped me back to my house. I broke to pieces on the kitchen floor and couldn't control my tears. My mind was doing somersaults and my thoughts had gone wild. I realised how isolated I had become, how alone I felt, and I just needed my dad. In this state of panic I called him and begged him to come back and get me. I was wearing ten layers, including a fleece Santa Claus onesie, topped with my huge leopard print fur coat. I looked like a big bundle of mess with my sunken yet swollen face, distraught, peeping out from under my hood. Black eyeliner was smeared all over my already tear-stained face. I looked like I had escaped from an asylum, shaking with cold, fear and tears.

My dad arrived, scooped me up, put me in the car and drove me round the corner to his hotel. I cannot even begin to imagine what the hotel receptionist must have thought when my tall, bald-headed dad returned with a deathly looking, hysterical girl wearing a santa outfit. I climbed into the bed in the hotel room and slipped in and out of consciousness between crying.

It was clear to REDS that I was lying in my food diary and not improving at all. My weight continued to drop pounds every time I stood on the scales. Every appointment went the same way... I was warned of the damage I was doing to myself, I was told that I was in a 'psychotic state', my body was eating itself, I was going to die, I needed to eat more and if I continued any longer like this I would be hospitalised. I would agree to everything they said and promise to try harder, knowing there was no way in a million years that I would actually do so. I sort of half convinced myself that 'I wanted to get better'. In reality though, I really didn't. I wasn't ready, I didn't choose to seek help from the eating disorders unit, I was made to... So the help they tried to give me, went ignored. It made my parents so happy when I expressed my desire to get back to my old self, but I didn't mean my old body, I just meant my old happiness.

I went home some weekends, once with my boyfriend. He and I went to meet one of my best friends in town for a coffee. I was freezing cold wrapped in as many layers as I could drape around my bones. I spoke so quietly that my friend could barely hear what I was saying. She knew that I was quite seriously ill, but because I had not seen her in so long, she got a horrible shock when she saw me; I could see it in her worried face. I felt so ill and out of it again, I had literally nothing to say.

I made the decision to go home a week before I was due to break up for the Christmas holidays, to recover over December and then return to University as normal, once I was ok. I had no idea that the average time of recovery for an eating disorder is seven years. How naive I was to be so sure I would be absolutely fine in the space of four weeks, when I was so sick that I was on the verge of death. I was oblivious to what I had got myself into and how it was going to affect the following years of my life.

My Mum was in Newcastle this time. We booked ourselves a flight to London literally a couple of hours before boarding the plane. I said goodbye to some of my friends, grabbed two bags of clothes and flew back home. I genuinely had no idea that this was the end of my University experience. Had I realised this, I would probably never have boarded that plane. But I would probably also not be alive today.

We were collected from the airport by Dad, who drove us home. The first thing I did once back, was pretend to go and have a bath. My parents didn't know that I was a smoker and so I hadn't had the chance to have a cigarette all day. I locked the bathroom door, turned on the water without the plug, and climbed out the window onto the roof. It was a blustery, stormy night and I felt lightheaded and dazed puffing on my cigarette, trying not to be blown away by the strong wind. I pulled myself back through the window with difficulty as I had such little strength left. I sprayed as much air freshener as I could, and revelled in the excitement of my secrecy.

Something I wrote in my phone on 8th December 2011 at 22:28:

Too much stuff just going on in my head. Everything's moving too quickly. On an exhausting pathway. I feel like a failure. I feel like a child. But like a senior. I'm not sure which works best. My head is full of things I want to do. Distractions to work. I want to pass so badly but I have no motivation it seems. By seeking motivation and inspiration it is further filling up my mind. Though it's inspiring it's also distracting. Too many things. I think my head might explode. I'm trying to be positive, and I am. But it's exhausting. The overwhelming feeling of guilt for being home because I can't cope, is quite embarrassing. I feel like I'm taking advantage? Though I know I'm ill, I don't feel right having to live back with my parents, wasting their money and time. I feel sad. Scared of life. I've disappointed so many people.

Chapter 9
SKELETAL MIND

9th December 2011

Dear Miss Davies,

We have received a referral from DR ******, consultant psychiatrist, at the Richmond Eating Disorders service in Newcastle. As confirmed on the phone this morning, I am writing with the following triage assessment appointment:

Monday 12th December 2011 at 9am with *****, senior dietician.

Please do not hesitate to contact me if you have any questions about the appointment.

Your sincerely

*****

I did not have any questions regarding the appointment, bar the obvious - why the hell did I have to go?

From the second I stepped into L****** House, I fucking hated it. It was a big cottage like building with an eerie and stagnant atmosphere. In general the whole place just gave me the worst vibes. It reminded me of the type of buildings I had visited my grandparents in when they were in old peoples' homes.

The receptionist was a nice, quiet lady, but I hated being kept waiting in that dull, silent room. Why was I always made to wait for appointments I didn't even want to attend? My dietician was the biggest fucking bitch I have ever met in my life. One might assume, and many did, that this was my illness speaking and that I felt this way about her for the obvious reason that she was going to try and make me eat. Yes, of course this did make me automatically dislike her, but I was fine with my Newcastle dietician. This lady was completely different. I will speak more about her later.

My days at home became a set routine which I followed religiously. I would wake up at half three in the morning to refill my hot water bottle and have a solitary cigarette in the pitch black garden. I liked these moments as the world was dark and silent, I was alone in the stillness of the night with my thoughts, uninterrupted. There was no chaos at that time in the morning; it was probably the only time I was able to feel calm, peaceful, unwatched. I was sleeping in thermal vests, tracksuits and under two duvets (and was still cold). I would sleep again until five or six before getting up properly. I would scuttle into the kitchen while the rest of my family were still sleeping and pretend to have breakfast. I was supposed to be eating a specific measurement of oats with chocolate soya milk. I would measure this exactly, before throwing the oats behind a tree in the garden and pouring the milk down the sink, washing away any traces carefully. I would mix a few tiny bits together in a bowl, taking extra care to smear the milk around to coat the spoon and splash a bit on the table (it had to look as realistic as possible). Once happy with my work I would leave my bowl and the remainders above the dishwasher, as a sort of 'look at me, I have eaten my breakfast' message to my parents. Silently smirking to myself, I got an incredible kick out of how realistic I made it look, and how stupid everyone was for not realising. The adrenaline rush from these games was crazy; I was high on lies, manipulation and success in beating the system. I found it hard to hide my grin after such sneaky tricks.

After 'breakfast', I would then retreat to the living room and lie on the sofa under duvets, scorching my skin again with my ever present hot water bottle. I would watch daytime TV, drink diet coke, chew 120 pieces of chewing gum per day and buy people presents online.

Lunch would be the lowest calorie thing I could possibly create without being so obvious. Another diet coke would be downed before I faced the difficult task of consuming what I had made. After this, back to the living room I went until it was supper at 5 o'clock, which would be pretty much the same as lunch. Bed would be around half six as I would be completely exhausted by the end of the day.

Although I was being made to eat a fair bit more than I had been surviving on at University, my body was in a state of crisis and starvation. It needed a hell of a lot more calories to halt or stabilise my weight loss, let alone increase it. When in starvation mode, your body literally eats itself; it is receiving no other source of fuel so it feeds off your fat, then your muscles, which physically waste away. This had happened to me and I was incredibly weak. I was literally just surviving on what was left of my body, so the amount of food I was eating was having basically no effect.

Being officially diagnosed with Anorexia Nervosa was a blessing and a curse. Obviously it is a huge curse altogether, but to know what was wrong with me and to have some kind of explanation as to why everyone kept telling me I was ill, was a kind of relief. The problem with obtaining the label 'Anorexia' though, is that it can lead to a dangerous way of thinking. I believed for sometime that I had to work extra hard now that I was wearing this badge of acknowledgement. I had to live up to this title. I could not possibly eat in front of anyone now incase they though

I wasn't actually anorexic and was just attention seeking. What if they thought I made it all up? It was due to this twisted theory and the habits that had become so ingrained in my mind that they were automatic, that I continued to drop weight, faster and faster.

Phone note, 19 December 2011 22.44

Feeling so successful but a complete and absolute failure. It's overwhelming to feel both of these emotions so fiercely at the same time about the same action. 1 step closer to recovery, but a rule has been broken. You've failed yet you're succeeding, but really you've failed. Never ever do that again. That's a tiny step you're gonna have to take every day - it's nothing. No fucking way are you doing that again. So disobedient. Why did you do it. To recover. Why not something else. Why something else.

I am perfectly aware that this note probably makes absolutely no sense to you. To be honest I find it tricky to translate myself, but I know the message I was trying to convey through it. The way that passage is worded demonstrates very vividly the split personality that I was experiencing. The choice of decisions: to get thinner, or to get better, half of me wanted one thing but half of me wanted the other. In order for me to separate myself from my illness, I had to learn to pick up on when it was 'real Lydia' talking (thinking), and when it was ana (anorexia). The: 'never ever do that again', is a prime example of the running commentary I had in my head. It was a voice that came and went, sometimes more viciously than others. It shouted at me, insulted me, and tore my self-worth to pieces.

It is clear to see from that extract that I really was not with it anymore, my head was way, way up in the clouds, a thick mist surrounding my already confused brain. My memory had evaporated to nothing, I didn't know what month it was, let alone what day. I found it difficult to express my theories so that people could understand them; to them I was just jabbering a jumbled mess of words that made little or no sense. Writing this section, I feel similar, as I genuinely had lost my mind at this point, so although I know what happened and a lot of things are very vivid for me to remember, my accuracy of the exact order of events, dates and times are skewed. When you starve your body to the extreme, you also deprive your brain of vital nutrients. I had not been able to concentrate on anything for a long time anyway, but this was on another level. I could not focus on TV, keep a conversation going, type anything that made sense, or even read. It is this starvation effect on the brain, that body dysmorphia feasts off . You're head is so messed up that when you look in the mirror you see a fat, hideously ugly girl staring back, when to everyone else you look like you have been starved to death. My eyes would be magnetically drawn to every non-existent flaw of fat on my emaciated body. I wanted to be a human clotheshorse, as light as a feather floating in a soft breeze, as delicate as an autumn leaf, as pure as as I could possibly be. No matter how light the scales said I was and how terrifyingly thin I got, I still saw fat, I still saw room for improvement and I knew I was capable of it. The intense urge to go further, to push my limits as far as I possibly could, to keep going until I could go no more, was overpowering and so, so addictive.

Even when there were moments that I could see that actually I WAS thin, I knew that if I had got so far, I could go further. My determination (a trait I have always been told I possess), was really not beneficial to me in this instance, as it made me keep going and going. I had not finished my competition with myself yet and being the determined girl I had always been, I would keep pushing myself to my absolute limit.

Chapter 10
THE HOLY PARSNIP

It was almost Christmas and I was full of festivity and excitement - the pretty lights, the cheerful atmosphere, the giving, the loving, the smell of the pine tree and mulled wine. I could not wait to give everyone the special presents I had been buying since October.

When you become as sick as I was and know there is a possibility that you will not awake from you next sleep, you learn to appreciate every tiny detail a million times more than you ever have before. When people argued or shouted I genuinely found it impossible to understand how or why. There was nothing to argue about, everything was so amazing. I wanted to spend as many seconds as possible with the people that meant the most to me. I wanted to show them how much I love them through generosity, kindness and compassion.

On Christmas day my family piled into the car and drove to my Aunt's house in London. The sparkling white kitchen was bursting with laughter and happiness from cousins, aunts and uncles. Everyone was sipping on champagne and feasting like kings. Obviously, Christmas dinner can be one of the most daunting times of the year for someone suffering with Anorexia. I had brought a tupperware with me containing spinach and cold tinned tomatoes. Sitting round the huge table, brimming with food and excitement, everyone overeating the delicious feast, piling their plates high and complementing the wonderful tastes, is a horrible feeling for someone who is literally unable to eat. I was painfully thin and the copious amounts of champagne on my empty stomach had gone straight to my head. I felt so envious and bitter that they could all be so happy and relaxed whilst eating their weight in calorie rich food. I felt very left out, which prompted me to make a really drastic decision.... I was going to try a parsnip.

I picked one out of the bowl in the middle of the table and dropped it into my tupperware, examining the coating of honey and oil. I took a tiny bite, and oh my god, it was incredible. I ate the whole holy parsnip piece, then proceeded to pile another eight onto my plate, just like that, out of absolutely nowhere. I genuinely had never tasted anything so amazing in my life than that sacred, honey glazed parsnip. I cannot even begin to describe the sensations, but I was in heaven... I guess I had deprived myself of food for so long and made sure that everything I did eat was horrible, that any food would have tasted amazing. I ate more and more of them, my family staring at me in both amazement and shock. I then asked for more and my dad suggested that I might have had enough and should probably stop. I stared at him, completely mortified, face burning red. I flew into a silent fury, ran upstairs and cried my eyes out, utterly humiliated. I rang my boyfriend, in tears, for comfort, then fell asleep for a few hours and missed most of the afternoon due to exhaustion as I wasn't used to leaving the house.

It is a horrible, horrible feeling to have everyone begging and pleading with you to eat more constantly, only to have those same people tell you to stop eating when you feel as though you are finally discovering the pleasure in food again. It was awful and so embarrassing. I understand that they guessed how bad I would feel after consuming so much more than usual, and they were probably trying to spare me from the painful emotions that would inevitably follow. I just didn't understand how they decided and assumed they had the right to tell me not to eat, after telling me to eat for so long, after crying to me about it all those times. I was dying of starvation for god sake, all I ate was a few damn parsnips; they're all over double what I weighed and had been stuffing their greedy gobs all day with piles and piles of fatty food. How dare they, how fucking dare they! I was furious.

I would class this parsnip incident as my first binge, and there were many more to follow.

Many people with anorexia, once in recovery, go on to develop bulimia and vice versa. Though they are very different disorders, they connect with an unbreakable link: both using food in some way as a coping mechanism. An affair with bulimia when you have anorexia is seductively tempting, getting the best of both worlds. It is extremely common to swing back and forth between the two illnesses, creating a chaotic mess in the sufferers mind through such contrasting behaviours. And swinging between the two is exactly what I went on to do later.

Christmas over and done with, I continued to drop more weight. My parents were desperately worried to the point where they were coming into my room during the night whilst I was asleep to check my pulse. They told me they were terrified to open my door in the mornings incase I hadn't survived another night.

Cognitive behavioural therapy with my same old therapist began again, in an attempt to tackle the mental side of my illness. I loved going to my appointments with him because he was so understanding. He was actually interested in what I had to say and his methods of treatment interested me. My appointments with him were the only opportunity I got to express myself completely, about how I actually felt and what I was thinking. I trusted him and felt a strong sense of connection and security.

Another big reason I loved these appointments was purely because they got me out of the house for a couple of hours, which was an ever-diminishing opportunity. My driving licence had been confiscated as my BMI was so low that it would be very dangerous to drive incase I fainted or collapsed or whatever). This left me completely housebound. I was furious. Also my mind was so fucked that I was apparently in no position to make justified decisions, which could jeopardise the safety of others. This makes perfect sense to me now, but at the time it really didn't.

The last great thing about my appointments was that I got weighed. Like I mentioned earlier, we did not own scales which was a horrible situation for me to adjust to. I was so used to watching the numbers drop on the scale, and checking on an almost hourly basis at University; sneaking into my friends bedroom when everyone was out, to stand on that thing. I would crave seeing what that number would tell me; it would define my mood, my way of thinking, my actions, and my day. It meant everything and I found it difficult to cope without it.

Week by week at these appointments, I watched the number drop further and further. I was delighted, as I was so sure I must have gained weight since being home and eating more than before. The scales used in most medical appointment were in kgs, not stone, which was pretty tricky for me to grasp at first as I had always used stone. My iPhone was a permanent extension of my arm, so I would frantically convert the reading the second I saw it, so I could analyse how I was doing and what it meant.

In the sessions we talked about being mindful, as well as having in-depth conversations about my thoughts and feelings. They allowed me to use my brain and exercise my intellect which was very important to me, as I was feeling useless for the vast majority of time. We thought along very mutual wavelengths and I found the way he spoke to me fascinating. He treated me like a person, not a patient, and that was so important. When you are constantly treated like an ill person by everyone around you and told you are sick, in a psychotic state, you begin to believe that is all you are. It is a horrible feeling to be treated by everyone like a two year old when you are in fact twenty years old. I became very attached to our appointments, much to the disappointment of my Eating Disorders Unit.

Eating Disorder Units prefer all treatments to happen under one roof. This is so they can monitor precisely what is going on with the patient, not get any crossed wires and not develop any separations within the treatment plan. The fact that I was causing this separation and was adamant that I would continue my treatment exactly how I wanted, irritated and worried them greatly. The fact that they didn't like it, made me like it even more, because I didn't like them. It was another victory for me over their stupid system.

The next great event in my life was New Year's Eve. Being so weak, there wasn't a whole lot I could do. I invited three friends over for a meal that I cooked (ironically), before heading to Reigate, the local town. At the bar I ordered a Malibu and Coke for my friend and a Malibu and Diet Coke for myself. The lady gave me the drinks and I asked her if she would kindly put a wedge of lime in each. She returned with the drinks and I asked her which was which. She didn't know. I stared at her in horror as if she had just killed someone. I said that I was allergic to full fat Coke and needed to know which one was diet. She couldn't care a less and refused to make me another one. Angry tears of rage brimmed in my furious eyes. Why was this woman ruining my life and my night like this? I protested and argued with her until my brother came to my rescue. By this point I was extremely upset, very worked up and anxious, surely she could SEE that I wasn't going to drink a full fat coke? Her only suggestion was that I tried them, which was obviously out of the question. Three different people tried them and decided which was which, but this was just not enough for me. My brother comforted me as I shook with rage, and calmly explained to the people behind the bar that they needed to make me another drink. Reluctantly they did, but the rest of my night was tainted by the attitude and lack of sympathy from this bar woman.

Pretty much as soon as it chimed midnight I was more than ready to go home. I was used to going to bed at around six o'clock so was completely exhausted. The combination of alcohol, the diet coke ordeal, general lack of energy and two of the friends I went with walking off and leaving me, waiting in the car with my brother for forty minutes, freezing and shattered, had made this night a draining experience. I woke up the next day to the hangover of all hangovers. I felt so weak on the outside and inside. My liver genuinely hurt and every organ and limb of my body ached like it never had before.

Chapter 11
LETTING GO OF LOVE

2012

Phone note 31st December 2011 00:03

NY resolutions

Less drink - twice a week
Start French an hour a day
Go on walk every other day
Hour of Magazine each day
Blog everyday
Take an interesting picture each day
Less gum

I think it is pretty safe to say all of these resolutions got broken on the 1st January 2012. I continued to make and break unrealistic promises that I made to myself throughout the year.

While 2011 had been a fast and furious roller coaster of emotionally turbulent experiences, 2012 happened in slow motion. The road to recovery is time consuming, difficult and exhausting. It is a dull process in comparison to the whirlwind of adrenaline that pulled me down into the depths of the illness.

I had not seen my boyfriend since early December; he had a lot of work to do for University and then spent Christmas and New Year with his family and friends. We lived so far away that once I moved home it was difficult for us to see each other. Me going to see him at Uni was sadly out of the question. I would have to get public transport and stay and I just wasn't strong enough; the doctors wouldn't allow it. It would also mess up my strict eating plan that I wasn't following and interfere with all my appointments. This meant that it was down to him to travel down when he could and stay with me at my parents' house. It was the first week of January that he came to visit and I was so excited. We had spoken on the phone most days, but I really missed him. When he arrived we hugged so tight that it was painful.

Over the days he stayed, I became more and more withdrawn and distant. My body resembled that of a twelve year old boys, not the twenty year old woman he had previously been with. My mind too had changed. I didn't want anyone to hug me, touch me, come too close to me. At night, I wanted to be alone, sleeping in the exact position I always slept in, dreaming my amazing dreams, listening to my exact playlist. After adapting to this life and routine for almost a month, I was used to being alone...

Suddenly having another body beside me, arms wrapping around me, breath on my shoulder, eyelashes blinking against my skin, terrified me. I couldn't help it and believe me I tried. I didn't want to feel like I did, but I was used to isolating myself completely, living inside my own head and not letting anyone past my barriers. I could feel that something had changed and although I desperately wanted to change it back, I didn't know how. It was my illness.

I started to become snappy, uptight, and maybe even nasty. It wasn't me; but the snake like words that flicked off my tongue and flinches in my body when he touched me became more obvious to myself, more difficult to hold back. Every time I snapped at him for asking if I was ok, or darted to the other side of the sofa because he tried to hug me, I felt so incredibly guilty. He was unbelievable for standing by me like he did; I can't say I know many nineteen year olds who would have done the same. He was there for me unconditionally, and I will always remember and be truly grateful for that. I could not understand why I was being so harsh at the time, but I now realise it was because the illness had taken over me completely. I loved him with everything but became unable to express this whilst being suffocated by the disease.

I ended up taking pictures of my grotesque body in the mirror, wearing nothing but underwear, and showing him one night. I did this because I didn't think he understood the extent of how severely ill I had become (even though I know he did understand, probably more than me). I wanted to show him so that he could see with his own eyes, why I was appearing to push him away, why I didn't want a hug, why a hug hurt me. I remember vividly, how absolutely horrified he was when I showed him the pictures. The gap between my thighs was huge, with each tiny purple leg completely wasted away, no fat, no muscle, just bone. My hips jutted out, as did my rib cage, with my waist barely there. My angular skull propped up on my skinny neck. The photos from behind, were just bones. My bumpy spine protruding through my pasty skin, my pelvis accurately showing every detail of it's bone structure, the knife-sharp edges of my shoulders, my knees protruding from the rest of my legs. Even I could see that these pictures were horrifying.

My boyfriend and I went to the pub one evening to meet my oldest friend Libby and a friend of hers who was visiting from Germany. I could read the shock on their faces like a book when they saw me, but we all ignored the situation. We were having drinks and got onto the topic of my weight loss. Libby had been at the end of many 'phone calls from me while I was spiralling downhill. I remember a long conversation we had about a can of sweet corn when I was in Newcastle. I was terrified I had eaten too much, but she assured me from the other end of the phone in

Cardiff, that I needed to get some serious help if I thought this. Libby had been there for me through every stage of my life since I met her, aged 11. I have so many incredible childhood memories of us.

She expressed her worry to me and questioned why I was not getting better. I had seen her before Christmas when I moved home to recover, but had only got worse since then and she was vividly distraught by this. The night became a complete disaster, as I had no answers to the questions I was being asked. I wanted to be thin, that was it really, that had become my life, my reason for living. Libby burst into tears and said she was going to go home as she couldn't sit there any longer. Her German friend then also started crying. I felt annoyed as I felt my boyfriend was answering questions on my behalf. I most definitely had selective hearing but all I could hear was him saying: "she feels this, she did this, she feels like...". I was my own person and this was MY illness and Ana definitely didn't want me to share it with anyone else. When he said kind things like: "Lyds, we will get through this together", it made my cold blood boil. I was so protective over the disease, I couldn't even contemplate anyone else getting involved, or even giving me advice. How dare they when I am the one who got here and achieved this, anorexia is MINE, and I am hers. My boyfriend admitted to me that he wanted to be the 'knight in shining armour', so to speak, to be the one to rescue or save me from the grips of my illness. I couldn't bear to even listen to this idea, if anyone was going to turn me around, it was going to be me, by myself, with no one else. Reading this paragraph back is quite difficult as I now see that all of those thoughts came from the illness and not from myself. I would never feel those things now, and since recovering, I am far more able to see how my illness affected those around me... But to stay accurate to my story and demonstrate how mind altering anorexia can be, I've kept this passage in, because sadly that was exactly my thought process at that time.

There was one drunken night where we began to argue about my illness; I became so upset that I said I needed to sleep on my brother's floor because only he understood me. I remember feeling so guilty coming downstairs the next morning, seeing my boyfriend sitting on the sofa in our family living room, in the dark, where he had stayed all night, all because of me, all because of fucking anorexia.

It became apparent to me that I could not have both a boyfriend and anorexia. The main relationship in my life was now sadly, my illness; it was the other half of me, quite literally as I had become so deeply involved. My boyfriend got pushed out and was not included in my partnership with anorexia. I now truly appreciate how horrible a time it must have been for him and will always feel eternally sorry for what I put him through. I cannot stress enough how amazing he was (and I am sure still is). The thing is, I loved him so much that I didn't want him to have to go through any more. It was not fair on him to have to travel to see his sick girlfriend, only to be snapped at, pushed away and essentially unappreciated. I couldn't cope with the guilt of taking him away from the fun he should have been having in his first year of Uni, like I got to have: no responsibility, no stress, no illness, just fun. He deserved better than what I could give him at the time and I recognised that, through the fog in my brain. I decided I needed to sacrifice our relationship and let him go, for the sake of his happiness. Personally, I would have gladly kept going until I was better, but I didn't know if or when I was going to be better and in my mind that simply was not a fair thing to put someone through, even if they wanted to be there. I felt like I was holding him back and so for those reasons alone, my illness and I made the regretful decision to let go.

Once I eventually did begin to recover around six months later, in selfish hindsight, I truly regretted my decision. I was suddenly devastated at this point, having previously been completely indifferent and un-phased when it happened, when Ana controlled me. It's not because I wasn't upset, it's just that my emotions and perception of reality had become so warped and numbed due to my main focus, anorexia. The pain and upset for the loss of him which I should have experienced at that time, was muted until later, when my emotions began to come back and I wasn't completely consumed. I knew I was too late and that it was imperative that I accepted that what I did was the correct thing to do at that time, considering the complicated circumstances. I also had to accept that it was him who I had put through a horrible time and that he probably did have to deal with some emotions of his own. I told myself to respect that and to learn to live with the decision I had made all those months ago, even if I found it very difficult.

Chapter 12
I WATCH YOUR SPIRIT BREAK AS IT SHATTERS INTO A MILLION PIECES

18th January 2012

Dear Dr ********,

Diagnosis: Anorexia Nervosa (restrictive sub-type)

Medication: Nil

BMI: 12.6

Management plan:

1. To see GP for ECG this week.

2. Further appointment with *****, senior dietician, for review Friday 20th January 2012.

3. Had further appointment with myself on Monday 23rd January 2012 to refer for Day Care.

4. Had day care preparation appointment on Tuesday 24th January 2012.

5. Encouraged to eat regular meals and snacks with gradual increase in volumes.

6. Encouraged to cut down on chewing gum and diet coke as this will exacerbate her feeling of bloating.

7. Lydia to attend A&E if physically unwell out of hours.

8. Lydia and her parents to call L****** House Eating Disorders Service during office hours for advice/support.

Level of medical risk: High

I just wanted to update you on Lydia's progress since her referral to our service. You will have received details of the assessment carried out by ****, Senior Dietician, on 12th December 2011. I have met with Lydia twice now, the first time on 11th January 2012 and again on 16th January 2012. She is really struggling to make changes to her eating pattern and continues to insist on following a vegan and gluten-free diet. Physically she is very frail. She was just about able to do the SUSS test and struggled to get up from squatting, but did not lose her balance. Her temperature was 36.2oC though she was peripherally cool to touch with some redness of her fingers, but no edema. She had enlarged appearance of her parotid glands bilaterally and was chewing gum vigorously.

I understand that she has been seeing a private psychologist, **** ******, for CBT on and off since last summer and she reports finding this helpful. Unfortunately, however, her weight is continuing to slip down without evidence of stabilisation at all. I have spoken with her about various options including:

1. Her attending day care.
2. Her being referred for voluntary inpatient admission.
3. Her being referred for admission as an involuntary patient under a section of the Mental Health Act.

She was not keen on any of these options and insists that she is able to improve her health herself, despite evidence of her last few months being to the contrary.

Lydia allowed her mother to join us at our last appointment. Mum expressed a significant concern about her daughter's state of health. Mother reports finding it difficult to support Lydia to eat as Lydia refuses to eat what her mother makes, even if it is gluten-free and vegan. Mum is surprised at the level of continued weight loss, though Mum did go on to disclose that Lydia had gone to Brighton on the train at the weekend to get a tattoo, and increased level of activity may have contributed to the weight loss. Mum also expressed concern about Lydia's drinking - she is drinking a glass of wine at night - and her level of smoking - Lydia has picked up the habit of smoking and *had told her mother that she can only eat if she is allowed to have a cigarette afterwards.*

Following further discussion about the options open to Lydia, she is amenable to attending day care preparation appointments, though she believed that she is going to be able to stabilise her weight loss and show that she can gain weight as an outpatient over the next two weeks, and that actual admission for day care will therefore not be necessary. She is aware that if she is unable to halt the weight loss then the level of medical risk may be such that inpatient hospital admission is unavoidable.

I will keep you informed of her progress.

Yours sincerely,

Dr ****** ***
Consultant Psychiatrist

This was a copy of the letter I received following probably my worst appointment. I was so frail that I was barely able to walk. A healthy BMI is between 20 and 25, 18 and below are considered underweight, 16 and below prompts diagnosis of anorexia (although these guides vary from person to person). I was in an extremely dangerous place and death was a real risk. My heart could just stop beating at any minute, and although I was aware of this, it didn't really scare me.

At this particular appointment, I should really have been sectioned under the Mental Health Act. I have always been an extremely persuasive person, even as a child, so somehow managed to weave my way out of it, promising that I would improve and that hospitalisation was not an option. My mum was distraught at the thought of me being sectioned.

I was outraged that they thought I was mad. I thought I was much more clever than all of them put together. They were all older than me, but I had seen and experienced so much, that I believed I had a higher knowledge of the world. I could see things in different ways to everyone, in ways that I could not explain and they would never be able to understand even if they tried. They were stupid and I hated them for classing me as 'psychotic'. This is a word that was often used to describe me when I was attempting to explain my logical theories to the Eating Disorders Unit. Maybe they were just idiots and couldn't understand me because my level of intelligence and perception was superior to theirs, or that is what I believed at the time anyway.

To be accused of being mad is something else. To be told you are going to die, however, is ok if the facts add up and the sum is realistic. But to be told you are mad? How can you measure madness? Everyone is different and everyone thinks differently, therefore I find judging madness a little like judging art. My mind was an abstract work of art, a collage of colours and ideas. Their minds were like textbooks, boring, structured and unimaginative.

In the car on the way home after this appointment, my mum cried silent tears and I stared out the window, blankly. I didn't want to see her cry, especially not because of me. Half way home the song, 'Up' by James Morrison, came on the radio. It was pouring with rain and we were driving down the gloomy motorway. The lyrics of the song hit both of us and we both knew it. The song to this day still brings back vivid images and memories of that car journey...

How can I find you
When you're always hiding from yourself
Playing hide and seek with me
Till it gets too dark
Too dark, inside your shell
Why do I even try
When you take me for granted
I should know better by now
When you call I already hear that crashing sound
As it all falls down

It's never too late to turn it back around
Yeah I know you can
Don't bury your demons in the ground
When it all falls down
The only way is up, up, up
The only way is up

I watch your spirit break
As it shatters into a million pieces
Just like glass I see right through you
And your parade of excuses
Feels like groundhog day
You say the same things over and over
There that look in your eye
And I hear that crashing sound
As it all falls down

It's never too late to turn it back around
Yeah I know you can
Don't bury you demons in the ground
When it all falls down
The only way is up, up, up
The only way is up

It's your love that's strong

It's the only thing that keeps me holding on
It's your heart that's weak
But it's not too weak to bring you back to me

It's never too late to turn it back around
Yeah I know you can
Don't bury you demons in the ground
When it all falls down
The only way is up, up, up
The only way is up

That song was played at the perfect moment; it spoke to both of us as if it had been played then for a purpose, a reason. This moment in time was rock bottom for me; if I was any more sick I would have been dead. I was so ill, kept saying I wanted to get better, but just continued to do the opposite. Whether that was intentional or not, I cannot tell you. I guess half of me wanted nothing and the other half wanted my life back, and I remained trapped in the middle.

Chapter 13
ENLIGHTENMENT

Phone note 17th January 2012 21:32:

Reached the point of being sectioned
Bone marrow failure
Death risk (I am about to die)
There you go, you can do it. Well you've done it. Now get better!
Affecting about ten people in one night
Don't want dad to have a heart attack
Want mum to be able to sleep
Want friends not to worry
Polish girl ran out crying
Friends parents upset
Upsetting everyone
Get better
Be determined
Eat more
Have life
Be stylist
Eat snacks
Write down
Enjoy life
Stop wasting time

Do it
I look anorexic now
That's silly
You've been there
And done it
Now let's live

I now knew that I was going to die or be tube fed in a mental hospital against my will if I did not act fast. I became aware that my life had turned to shit and that I had lost everything. I had lost my independence, my degree, my education, my passion, my boyfriend, several friends, my identity and basically everything that meant something to me, besides my dedicated family and some close friends.

I was at the cinema one evening watching Warhorse and drinking Prosecco. Throughout the film, I would keep going in and out to smoke and think. I was standing outside the cinema, smoking in the rainy darkness. A switch flicked in my mind and a feeling of euphoria surged through my body. I had an epiphany and made the decision all of a sudden, to actually get better. I nearly fainted with this incredible feeling and had to lean back against the wall with a gigantic smile across my face that I could not wipe away. My mind was spinning with thoughts of getting better, being strong, beating this disease that had torn everything away from me. I would not let it rip away any more than it already had. This was it - I was ready to fight and beat this bitch. It was a sort of 'what the hell am I doing' realisation. I had achieved MORE than my goal of weight loss and was left with nothing. I thought to myself simply: 'I have done it, I have been there, it is time to get a life.'

Though I pinpoint this as a key turning point in wanting to recover, it really was not as simple as just eating more and getting better. Habits and rituals that had developed over time through the illness were completely ingrained within my being and would take time and effort to change. This was however, the spark that was to slowly burn through my estranged mind until explosion. Leaning against that wall, I genuinely felt as though I had reached Nirvana, a state of pure enlightenment which I don't know how else to describe. I went back into the cinema buzzing, and had no idea what happened in Warhorse. I spent the rest of the film writing notes in my phone of plans to recover and how I was going to do it by myself.

Phone note 19th January 2012 05:27:

The power cut was symbolic to my recovery I think. When the power was turned back on I could make my first bowl of porridge and start turning my power back on.

Mentally:

Its 5am. I'm feeling so anxious about breakfast. Although I know Im doing it and I should - of course weight gain is such a scary thought. My body physically changing is such a scary prospect. When I used to get scared my boobs were shrinking away, it's the same scared now that they will be growing. I just need to think, yeah but I want my fertility.

Now I know other people will be made so happy. But I feel that like by just eating I'm letting them down, cos won't they just be like errr, so she can eat - what an attention seeker - why didn't she just do that before.

Physically:

My stomach is hugely bloated and feels packed full. It's pretty painful if I'm honest. That's where the voice may kick in and suggest that eating is wrong. It did a bit last night. And it is a bit right now. It's asking me why I am going against all these ways and habits we have created, to feel agony in your stomach?! So yeah, the prospect of all the calories and carbs I'm going to have tomorrow is somewhat terrifying.

But if I don't gain weight I'll die so it's ok. I will have all the calories and do this.

I decided that night that I was going to eat breakfast. After not eating it for two years this was a massive alteration and breakthrough in my behaviour. I decided upon porridge made with oats and soya milk, with cinnamon, blueberries, banana and maple syrup. There was a power cut when I awoke that morning. I had to wait an hour and a half before I could prepare my much anticipated breakfast. The anxiety and nervous energy built up as I sat with my mum in the candlelit kitchen. I had to ignore the voice saying that the power cut happened as a signal for me not to eat, which was excruciatingly difficult. I ate it all and it made me feel so sick. I had not eaten that early in so long and was not used to my stomach having anything in it until at least 12pm. I felt bloated and strange all morning and could not feel comfortable with what I had done.

Lunch that day consisted of spicy parsnip and carrot soup (though I admit I didn't eat enough). I had my first snack that day too and my mum actually cried with joy when I decided that I was going to have a handful of vegetable crisps and a tablespoon of hummus. I wanted to kill myself after.

My first real supper in two years was half a ready meal vegetable curry (my old favourite), rice (which I picked at), spinach and a glass of Prosecco.

This day was the most traumatising, nerve wracking and generally uncomfortable day ever. I felt full, fat, greedy and horrible. Every negative comment I could come up with about myself was shouted at me in my head. Although I knew I was doing it to avoid being sectioned and to get my life back, it was still the most painful day in the world.

I went out for evening drinks of Prosecco and cider. I came home and ate another handful of crisps and a spoonful of guacamole. I cannot describe how much of an advance in progress that day was and I still don't know how I forced myself to do it.

Phone note 20th Jan 2012 06:21:

Its 5.30am. I'm walking round the house feeling really anxious. I've been awake for at least three hours worrying about breakfast. Not worrying that I am going to struggle really, more that I just don't want it.

I'm feeling pretty sad. Just looked through my mum's diary at the weeks and weeks ahead I'm gonna have to be at home doing nothing but focusing on this. And the amount of appointments, argh. Fuck that, I should be at Uni having fun. I wish this had never happened to me and my life hadn't been taken over. It's been two days where I've eaten the meals and it genuinely feels like it's been two weeks worth of food, cos it's so tiring physically and mentally.

Choosing what to have, the anxiety of whether that's right, what's a normal snack, what's the right portion to be healthy, what's the right portion to stabilise, what's the right portion to gain, how quickly will I gain, when will my legs stop feeling so weak, when will I experience hunger again. It's all such a time consuming process. That's why I'm feeling so sad it's happened. Because now I want to be better... getting better is going to take as much time, if not more, as getting this ill did. I suppose the only thing I can do is use this sadness to spur me on and ensure there is no relapsing. Because that will take away more of my life than has already been snatched away.

This sudden positive mindset continued for a while. I was excited telling my CBT therapist about my desire to recover and of the ideas I had thought up in order to help myself get there. I decided to take a photograph of every meal and snack I ate and turn it into a recovery coffee table book. He thought it was a magnificent idea and I was so pleased! It further fuelled my positivity and I believed I could do this. Contradicting this support however, was the reaction of the Eating Disorders Unit when I informed them of my great plan. My dietician's reaction was soul destroying and threw me straight back into a negative rage.

I felt like there was no pleasing these people. They consider me as a series of numbers, a patient number, a BMI score, weight, temperature, calorie count. They dehumanised me to the form of digits. It was so disheartening and even my mum was saddened by their reaction.

Blog post about the dietician:

VENOMOUS AND ANGRY.
The dietician:

I hate this woman. Like I absolutely hate her. I'm pretty easy going and open minded to everyone. Though I'd say I am quite a good judge of character, I'd never judge anyone before I knew them, because that is just closed minded.

Hate is a very strong word, and I can honestly say there is nobody else I know that I actually hate. This woman however, this condescending, patronising, evil bitch of a woman. The way everything she says, she does is in an irritating patronising whisper, staring pitifully at me as if I am about to die. The way she nods as if she's taking in what I am saying, although she is looking me up and down as I speak (again looking like she is about to burst into tears). The way she fucking makes me sit there for an hour

and gives not one ounce of encouragement for the progress
I feel like I have made, but instead asks why I am chewing
gum. WHY THE FUCK NOT. LIKE WHAT THE FUCK.
I am twenty years of age, I am allowed to chew some
chewing gum if I want to. WHY DO YOU WEAR
PURPLE EEEEEVERY FUCKING TIME I SEE YOU??
(Occasionally teal) and I did say this to her. She didn't like
it. She went bright red and patronisingly whispered, 'that's
not relevant now Lydia really is it' (followed by the nod
and the sad expression). ER well neither is the fact I've got
a piece of gum in my mouth. Who would want to spend
twenty minutes talking about that, what a waste of my
time.

She also undoes every single thing I say. She tells me I
am in a psychotic state and that nothing I am saying when
I am talking about why I want to get better makes sense,
WHEN IT DOES! She snatches my inspiration from me
every time I see her and makes me feel completely rubbish
and unmotivated.

Next time I see her I will say to her

"You are the least encouraging and the most
patronising beast of a woman I have ever met. The only
ounce of inspiration I gained from you and your sessions

was to get stronger so that I could ATTACK YOU, and
burn your hideous purple attire."

I was so close to saying this today but there was a
medical student sitting in my appointment, so I thought I
would save this for next time. I HAD BETTER GET
STRONGER FOR THEN.

As you can tell from this post I was extremely angry
and upset by this woman, crushing what I thought was the
ultimate breakthrough.

Chapter 14
COMPULSORY CUSTARD

Holidays over, my sister went back to boarding school, my brother moved to a flat in Brixton and my mum and dad went back to work. I remember looking at my mum's diary and feeling panicked about the pages of emptiness ahead for me. There was the occasional 'L - L****** House appointment', or 'L - blood tests', but apart from that, nothing. What was my life? How had this happened to me? I became extremely lonely and low in mood, to the extent where I thought I would be better off dead.

The conflict between the eating disorders unit and my cognitive behavioural therapist was growing. I told him that they were ignoring my psychological wellbeing and focusing solely on the numbers on the scales. How was I supposed to get better or feel better when they took no notice of my mental state and talked only of calories and weight gain. I told them that my work in CBT was by far the the most helpful part of my treatment and basically that they weren't helping me; their negative and dismissive attitudes were ruining my desire to return to health.

CBT therapist wrote to the Unit expressing concerns with their lack of sensitivity towards me as a person.

The response from L****** House was as follows:

Dear Dr ******

Thank you for your letter dated 4th February 2012 which Lydia hand delivered to me here at L******* House Eating Disorders service clinic. Lydia had given me permission to discuss her treatment at our service with you and with her consent I will arrange for you to be copied into correspondence to her GP.

Lydia is a very ill young woman and given the severity of her anorexia and her very low BMI score our treatment approach would include the prioritisation of weight restoration over psychological therapy at the start of treatment. This is because in our experience people at very low BMI often lack the cognitive ability to make use of psychological therapy at very low weights. It would also be my preference for Lydia to have all treatment for her eating disorder to be delivered within one service in order to reduce likelihood of splitting and also to ensure regular communication of risk and a multi disciplinary approach to the treatment and management of Lydia's eating difficulties. Lydia can access psychological support and therapy from within our service though currently she insists on continuing to see you privately and she apparently values quite highly the work you're doing together.

At her last review on 6th February 2012 Lydia made it clear her wish to continue to try and improve her nutritional health as an outpatient and she has turned down the Day care place that was offered to her. In my view she remains very disordered in her eating and her insistence on continuing with a vegan and gluten free diet despite the obvious physical risks to her health does concern the team and me greatly.

I have agreed on the following plan with Lydia and her mother who also attended part of the appointment.

1) Lydia agrees to continue to restore her nutritional health, expected weight gain of between 0.3 and 0.5kg per week.

2) If Lydia fails to meet this then in the first week she will be given an opportunity to rectify this. If she is unable to do so then Lydia agrees to be referred back to Day care and to attend. If she refuses to attend daycare she is aware that this will trigger a referral for hospital inpatient treatment on a voluntary or involuntary basis.

3) GP is to continue to check her bloods on a two weekly basis given her low BMI until further notice.

4) Lydia is to be weighed only by staff at the Eating Disorders Service. It is not helpful for Lydia to be weighted by her GP and by her therapist too as is happening at the present time.

*5) Lydia has arranged to meet for a review with ***** ****, Clinical Specialist Dietician, later this week possibly with her mother being present in order to discuss matters raised in your letter.*

6) It would be very helpful if you are planning to continue to work with Lydia that you are able to make yourself available to attend any reviews concerning Lydia's care.

Many thanks

Yours sincerely

*Dr ****** ****
Consultant Psychiatrist*

As mentioned in the letter above, day care was a serious option for my treatment. Because I was failing to make much progress by myself, I agreed to attend two introductory sessions.

My appointment was at 8am, so my mum and I got up and left the house by half six. It was still pitch black and pouring with rain. I was freezing cold and felt physically sick. I remember that morning so clearly, standing in the back garden in darkness smoking a cigarette, feeling tired and lifeless as I clutched my hot water bottle. Life felt painful and terrible right then. I definitely did not want to go to Daycare and I knew that I wouldn't. I had just agreed to go along to the inductions to please everyone, as they were all begging me to go. I was also a little curious to see what it was actually like.

Once we arrived I reluctantly pulled myself out of the car and went up three floors to the day care centre. I sat with my mum in the entrance in silence. There was a door at the end of the corridor with a glass window. I peered through in horror to see breakfast bowls and a trolley with tupperware boxes full of cereal, gallons of milk and juice. There were about eight painfully thin girls in the kitchen preparing their breakfast. I knew right then and there that there was absolutely no chance in hell of me going there. I thought they were all so much thinner than me! AND they were eating in front of each other? I couldn't even comprehend the idea of it.

A very nice lady took me into a private room to do my usual weight, blood, blood pressure, SUSS, BMI and all the boring stuff I had done one thousand times. I peeled away six of my eight layers to reveal my haggard body. The nice lady looked at me in amazement and said, 'I don't know how on earth you girls do it'. Naturally I took this as a compliment.

Next I had a meeting with their dietician, who took me through menu options for the week ahead. I had to choose from a list of (what I saw as) disgusting options to create a weekly food plan. They agreed to allow me soya milk and cereal bars rather than full fat milk and chocolate biscuits... But every single option on the menu contained cheese, which she said would not be altered for me. I was so disgusted.

The lunch options consisted of pasta based, cheese-infused meals, which as a gluten-free vegan, horrified me. As if this wasn't bad enough, I had to select dessert too, from a list of school-dinner-like puddings, with custard being compulsory. I was absolutely outraged - I HATE custard. Upon explaining this to the woman, she looked at me as if I was making excuses which she had heard many times before. I smiled sweetly and selected the least revolting things from the menu.

I decided that it would be unfair and illogical for me to attend this place. Because it is a voluntary day care centre, there are other people there who are actively trying to recover and that works for them. I knew that had I gone, I would have refused my food and refused to participate, which would create a difficult atmosphere for those who were trying hard to recover. I also knew that I would be constantly comparing myself to the other girls and attempting to compete with them. On top of that I was never going to sacrifice Veganism and start eating a ton of cheese every day. If I was going to increase my calories, I would do it with food I actually liked, rather than their cheese and custard-laden hospital food. So that was that idea out the window after just two appointments.

Though my parents urged me to go, I would not listen; this was my recovery and my decision and I would do it my way if I was going to do it at all, no one else's. The more it was brought up and suggested, the more I rejected the idea.

After the appointment, my mum and I went to a gigantic Tesco to buy food for the week. She was angry and frustrated with me, that after just telling Daycare I would broaden my food horizons and try harder, I picked up the same few staple items, including chewing gum and diet coke and refused to put anything else in the trolley. We drove home in silence, back at square one.

Through January and February I continued to struggle with eating. I was so set in my ways that I could not change them. I did gain a little weight, through panic infused binges late at night if I knew I had a weigh in the next day.

By mid February my weight was up a little. Although still incredibly low, this small increase managed to keep me out of hospital, away from being sectioned and very much in control of my own treatment plan, which is exactly what I wanted.

Since moving home in December, I had not been allowed to travel back up to Newcastle at all, even for a visit, as I was far too weak for the journey. I had only brought two small bags of things home with me on that flight and that was all I had until mid February. I missed my clothes, books, duvet and friends! I managed to persuade the unit to give my parents permission to drive me to Newcastle so I could collect my things and say a proper goodbye to my friends, as I was deferring my year of study to recover. They were extremely against the idea, which in turn made my parents very reluctant to take me. Luckily my sister had an interview at Newcastle University, so it all worked out quite well and we drove up for one night. I had arranged to meet all my friends in Spy bar, our favourite local. Being my usual negative self, I had thought that no one would turn up, but when I walked through the doors, I was amazed to see so many of them there. I felt like crying, and felt so incredibly lucky to have such supportive, understanding and amazing people in my life. My dad and sister came and joined in with the drinks after their meal. I felt so special and loved that night and it was one of the things that really pushed my mind in the right direction of wanting to get better, for all these people who cared. I will always remember that night and thank everyone who was there, for making it what it was.

Chapter 15
GIVE ME A REASON GIVE ME A JOY

13th March 2012

Diagnosis: Anorexia Nervosa

BMI: 15.9

Management plan:

1. To continue to see Dietician ******* **** every 10/7 for support and monitoring.

2. Further appointment with myself for review in 4-5 weeks.

3. To refer Lydia for assessment with Dr ****** for CBT - either for group or individual work now that her BMI is less critical.

4. It is Lydia's preference to continue to see Dr **** ****** Cognitive Psychotherapist for weekly sessions.

5. GP to reduce frequency of blood investigations to monthly. Her MCV is raised so may be helpful to check B12 and foliate when blood is taken next. Her WCC remains low at 3.1 indicating bone marrow suppression because of her low weight.

6. *She has asked if she can drive. Whilst the regulations suggest that it is not advisable for those with a BMI of less than 15 and Lydia is above this, I think it would be prudent to wait a few weeks given that she has only very recently made progress in restoring her weight to above this level.*

I wanted to update you on Lydia's progress.

*I met with her for a CPA review. Also present was ****** ****, Senior Dietician, Lydia's mother, and **** ******, her private therapist who has been seeing Lydia for some time now on a weekly basis.*

It was great to hear that Lydia has managed to improve her nutritional health as an outpatient, despite our concerns about her being able to do this as an outpatient, and is currently a BMI of just under 16. She has continued to eat a vegan and gluten-free diet. Whilst we are less concerned than previously about her medical risks, she does remain very eating disordered and continues to have a very narrowed repertoire of foods that she will eat and this rigidity does cause tensions in the house and with shopping, and also makes it difficult to enjoy food socially. I understand that Lydia continues to eat in a very restrictive fashion during the day and is bingeing on food in the evenings.

She is well engaged with her work with Dr ****** (CBT therapist), who kindly made the time to attend the CPA review. He informed me that his work is mostly based on Mindfulness based Therapy and food and eating are not discussed at all in the sessions. Lydia remains keen to continue with these sessions privately and expressed some reluctance to consider assessment for psychological work within the EDS as she does not want to change therapists. We would not recommend that Lydia see two therapists at the same time so we will need to think about this further once she has had an assessment with Dr. ******.

There had been some concern about Lydia's mood a few weeks ago. Lydia does feel low from time to time but it lasts for a matter of hours and she denies ever having had any suicidal thoughts when feeling this way. She finds it difficult to broach this topic with professionals, though would be able to answer honestly if asked directly how she was feeling.

Management plan as described above. I will keep you updated on her progress.

Yours sincerely

Dr ****** ***
Consultant Psychiatrist.

It was by this point that my affair with bulimia was getting more serious. What started out as just a little fun, gaining weight before my appointments to up my BMI, then fasting the rest of the week before repeating, soon turned into episodes of full blown, uncontrollable eating and purging. I found more and more frequently that once I began to eat, I literally couldn't stop. This was particularly prominent in the evenings and after the consumption of alcohol.

For someone who has been so strict with their diet and in control of every single bite they put in their mouth, going the opposite way entirely, and not being able to stop eating, is an extremely frightening happening to occur. I was assured by the EDS that the bingeing was purely a way of my body desperately trying to get the nutrients it needed so badly, as I had deprived it for so long. It was like every time I ate, my body subconsciously thought this could be the last time in a long time it would be allowed food, so it went all out. I was promised and assured that this would stop once I was of a higher weight / BMI.

Before I could realise it, I would have consumed an insane amount of calories. Sometimes I would eat so much in one go that I genuinely could not remember what I had eaten. It was as if I was attempting to fill a bottomless pit, no matter how much I had, it was never, ever enough. I could not fill my tiny stomach up, there was always room for more. After an episode like this, I would feel horrifically guilty and disgusted in myself. The next few hours would be spent downing pints of water and puking up my guts in a desperate attempt to rid myself of all the calories before they were absorbed. It was a race against time.

It was not uncommon for me to empty boxes of cereal out into the bin, so that I wouldn't be unable to eat it when a binge came on. Even so, when I got taken over I would find myself grabbing handfuls back from the bin and shoving them in my mouth. Because this didn't work, I started spraying foods with detox or deodorant before throwing them away, in a desperate attempt to prevent myself from eating. Even this didn't work and I would find myself picking every toxic piece of Special K back out during a binge.

I was painfully lonely. My days were spent in the house by myself. My mum and dad would go to work. I would watch daytime TV, drink wine for lunch sometimes instead of having food, if I was really bored, which in turn would cause me to binge on roasted vegetables and other food in the house, before legging it to the toilet to try and purge as much as I could before my mum got back from work. I was talking to myself, depressed and sat in my room in darkness alone, crying, curtains closed, duvet over my head. There was no point in anything to me. I didn't even know why I was getting up in the morning. All I was going to do was watch TV and eat too much, and for what?! It was an extremely dark stage of my life and I have never felt more isolated or alone as I did then.

I was also finding it very difficult to cope with the weight gain that the binging episodes were causing me. I was no longer doing it intentionally; I was an out of control mess and a million miles away from the routine and controlled lifestyle that I had so accurately perfected.

Routine is an important word within this context. When you take away routine, you take away purpose. When people are unemployed and struggling to find work for instance, it is not uncommon that they develop depression and a loss of motivation for life. I tried so many different techniques to improve this situation for myself, including creating timetables filled with activities and setting myself goals. Nothing worked though, as I knew none of it meant anything. Why would I want to draw for an hour? What was I even doing it for; it certainly wasn't going to get me anywhere in life. Everything seemed pointless to me and I slipped deeper and deeper into the vicious cycle of binging and purging - it was like it was all I had to do with my empty days.

For several months this was what my life consisted of. I was in a living hell, from which I could not escape. No matter how hard I tried, I was well and truly stuck and could not find a way out. I pencilled into my diary every time one of my friends was home from university and I would be able to slightly enjoy life briefly, though even these meetings usually turned into disaster. I remember one evening coming back from meeting a friend in Croydon. As I walked to the station to catch my train home, I passed a Waitrose and my feet marched me in, suddenly and automatically, hands grabbing, head changing. I got on the train and shovelled the food down my throat. Everyone around me was staring, but my tunnel vision could only see the food. I couldn't stop and was unable to give a shit until the pure humiliation kicked in after. When I reached my destination I wasn't finished, I wasn't ready to go home. Instead, I walked in the dark to the local corner shop, purchased more binge food and went and lay underneath a car at the station car park, in the pitch black. Once I reached the point where I could barely move, I rolled out and proceeded to vomit in the carpark, people walking past me, watching me make myself sick.

I could not look in the mirror; showering was difficult as seeing my naked, growing body disgusted me so much. I was constantly crying, deep in depression and trapped in my own chaotic world.

My parents tried their best to help me and suggested ideas for how to occupy myself. They pushed the idea of day care constantly to give me routine and to control my erratic eating habits better, but I still refused. I was fat now, so I was definitely not going to skinny school.

Phone note 30th Jan 16:58

I don't like recovery. Going through wanting to eat, eating, not wanting to eat, feeling sick, not knowing when to stop, wanting to get better, not wanting to be fat, feeling better, not feeling better, going up, going down, not sure why. I fucking hate it. I'm fucking sick of it. I want to be dead.

It was around this point that I started seriously contemplating suicide. I had no reason to live, no purpose in life, I was just there, miserable, making others miserable, and in so much pain mentally.

Phone note 31st Jan 2012 20:08

To all my friends and family and those closest to me. I am eternally sorry I was unable to find the strength and courage to fight my inner demons. I wanted to be better so badly for all of you because my love for you was indescribable. I don't want you to be sad. For you to be happy is my greatest wish. Don't waste time being upset. I wasted too much time, it's so precious. I will always be looking down on you and see you again one day where we can hug. Look after each other please and be happy. I want you to know I never meant for this to happen and I thank you and love you for all the support you gave me. It meant the world and I am eternally grateful. No one can help me though and no one caused this horrible disease. Remember that.

All of my love and peace and I will miss you all a ridiculous amount.

Love from your Lydia, xox

This was one of a few suicide notes I wrote during this period. There was one evening when my mum and dad were both out. I was having a few glasses of wine while watching Come Dine with Me. It was all such a lovely idea of a relaxing evening to myself. But then the binge monster entered me. I could not shake the thought away of all that tempting food in the kitchen, just two rooms away and the fantastic opportunity (what with my parents being out for the evening). I had to have it all. I ate so much it was ridiculous, loaves of bread, toast, bagels, boxes of cereal, soya milk, packets and packets of biscuits, whole jars of jam, nuts, crisps, cake, sauces. Afterwards, I genuinely could not believe what I had done. How could I, I was in disbelief, shock and just completely mortified. This only led me to the common mindset of 'oh you've done it now, you've ruined everything you fat pig, you're going to have to purge anyway so you may as well carry on'. So I continued my crazed eating frenzy until finally, the bottomless pit was filled to my throat, literally. I decided I had to be sick. By this point I was so exhausted that my gag reflex was not functioning as I wished. I tried everything: two fingers, three fingers, toothbrush, and all forced as far down my throat as far they would go. The sharp bristles of the toothbrush scratching against my oesophagus and prickling my tonsils, was agonising. After trying and failing for a good half hour, I chucked the blood stained toothbrush on the floor and decided I would have to try something else. I crept downstairs to the medicine cabinet. Inside was a pack of Nurofen, nearly all there. I swallowed a handful of them. I then swallowed my entire pack of antidepressants and an entire pack of laxatives. This cocktail of alcohol, excessive food and overdose of medication churned around in my stomach. In hindsight I took these pills for three reasons. First being, that perhaps they may induce vomiting. Second, maybe they would kill me and I would die and go to heaven and would not have to be in this horrific place I was stuck in any longer. Third, failing sick or death, perhaps if I was taken to hospital they would pump my stomach - then I would be able to get rid of all that food!

When my parents got home I wasn't dead, nor had I been sick, so option three had to be the one. I informed my parents of the evening's events and they were horrified. My mum rushed me to A&E. By the time we arrived I was fairly out of it: dopey, drowsy and pretty much fucked. We sat in the waiting room before I got admitted to a hospital bed. My mum sat beside me as I dosed. We could hear drunk people puking up violently on either side of the cubicle. My poor mum who has always hated sick had to sit there and listen. I just felt so jealous that all these people were throwing up so much and I still hadn't.

When the nurse attended to me, the first question I had was, "when are you going to pump my stomach?". I was asked all the details of the overdose, and she then decided that if they induced vomiting or pumped my stomach, it would do more damage than good, as it could cause internal bruising or bleeding. I burst into floods of tears and begged her to reconsider. The whole fucking reason I was there was to get rid of the thousands and thousands of calories that I had just consumed. I was not at all worried by the harm the pills could have caused me, nor the damage stomach pumping could do, I was only concerned about the binge sitting in my stomach, calories being absorbed by my horrible body by the second.

I spent the night in hospital. Every time I managed to drift off to sleep, a nurse would wake me up to take my blood pressure. I was attached to a drip which apparently had no calories (yes, that was my first question) and the tube was left hanging from my arm all night. My mum picked me up in the morning relieved that I was ok. I returned home still thinking about the horrific night (the binge, not the suicide attempt or the hospital admission). My poor parents were devastated that I had got to such an unhappy place. And once again urged me to go to Daycare. Once again, I refused.

25th May 2012

Dear Dr ********,

Diagnosis: Anorexia Nervosa
Co-Morbid Depressive features

BMI: 15.6

Management plan:

1. *Medication: to see GP recommencing Sertraline 50mg increasing weekly by 50mg to max 200mg if required (as the eating disorder service does not have access to prescribing budget we are unable to issue prescriptions for medications.)*
2. *Therapy: had an appointment to begin therapy with Dr ******* ****** - Clinical Psychologist within EDS on a weekly basis. Is also seeing dietician for nutritional support and advice.*
3. *Further appointment with myself in 10 days to review mood.*
4. *Advise Lydia to contact Richmond fellowship about looking for support in finding structure to her time.*

I reviewed Lydia in the clinic today. This was an urgent appointment arranged following contact with Lydia's mother who was concerned about Lydia's mood.

Lydia had been really struggling with feelings of self-loathing and hatred and this is being exacerbated by the binge episodes she is experiencing. She left a suicide note for her parents and was found by her mother with a plastic bag over her head recently prompting her mother to get in touch. She feels low all day every day and her concentration is poor as is her volition. She feels death would be a good escape from the anorexic thoughts and from facing the aftermath of feelings following a binge.

Lydia describes feeling quite low in mood without being able to see a future. She feels powerless to control the binge episodes and restricts the rest of the time. She struggles with sticking to the diet plan and feels her days are full of thinking about food. She is not driving and this restricts where and what she can do. She also has no structure to her days as many activities she has organised she either lost interest in or they fell through. She is also sad about the fact that she has not completed her degree because of the anorexia and today would have been the last day of her course.

Yours sincerely,

Dr ****** ***
Consultant Psychiatrist

I was sending myself mad through boredom and loneliness. To this day I have no idea how I got through those months. 'Straightforward' anorexia had turned into a cluster of destructive issues, which I faced on a daily basis. Depression, anxiety, anorexia binge-purge subtype, bulimia, suicide attempts and occasional self-harm were the most prominent features of my sad little life.

Each section that I have written, I state, is more difficult than the last, but this section genuinely is the most difficult to word.

Blog post 4th May 2012 09:53 pm

?

I find reality a mystery, a very difficult concept. The more days that pass the less real life seems. I have even found myself questioning whether life is actually a dream and dreams are actually life. Some days I am convinced I am going to just wake up and this time will have been a very long detailed dream. I say detailed, however I genuinely cannot remember much since August. August - present is somewhat of a blur. Yes I can remember elements of it but no detail, no feeling, nothing relevant. Each day I think might seem shorter ends up seeming never fucking ending! Tasks set and goals get broken far too frequently. Each hour becomes too long. Focus is impossible. Concentration is non-existent. I haven't a clue what is going on and I fail to remember anything that happened in the past hour, let alone the past day/month/year. I'm not sure what is more ridiculous, myself, life, or this blog post. Because NONE of them make any sense.

I have a strong feeling I should not post this because I sound genuinely mad. Fuck!

But I really couldn't give a fuck.

Although I was eating a lot more calories now, mainly in the form of binges, the voice in my head was stronger and more brutal than ever. There was a constant devil in my mind. I have never been bullied, but the bullying I was doing to myself was worse than any harsh comment anyone could say to me. I ripped my own self-esteem to shreds and had zero confidence. I was ashamed to be me and I wanted desperately to wear a balaclava whenever I left the house, so that no one would have to look at my hideous face and I could hide my humiliation beneath it. I wrote diaries and notes to myself constantly. Well, actually I didn't, the voice did. Reading them back the majority are in the third person, talking TO me, instructing me and insulting me. By eating again and gaining weight the illness was absolutely furious. Anorexia hissed violent and messed up things to me as bulimia messed up her plan.

Here are a few examples of notes that anorexia wrote in my phone to me, to remind me of what a repulsive animal I was:

19th Feb 2012 20:54:

Every mouthful adds fat
Try and only have three

20th Feb 2012 22:23:

I worked so hard
I want it all back. That's what I worked so hard for
before everyone ruined it. Now I'm so fat I can't even see
my hips. My big sides are creeping back. It took me years
and years to get rid of them. So happy when they were
gone. Fat and ugly when they are there. Burn calories
NOW.

10th March 2012 01:06:

You disgusting fat binging beast
No alcohol
Use the list
Nothing tomorrow
Bed

17th March 2012 00:30:

I feel lost, trapped, disgusting, helpless and irrelevant.
Tomorrow is a new day. Eating is not needed. If I eat,
something really bad will happen. Don't do it. You don't

*deserve it. Remember when you ate from the bin and you
binge every single day. Disgusting girl. Not again. It's
vile. Tomorrow is a new day. Be motivated and stay strong.
    Newcastle routine. Eat asparagus if famished.*

27th March 2012 22:21:

*Very simple.
Eat only raw, very small amounts on purpose.
Or you will be as fat as you used to be.*

Compare the pictures. Much fatter now. Much too fat.

*Eating is wrong for me. Deprivation is right. Be
confident in your ability and inner power. Power to say no
all the time.*

Cut out protein, carbs, oil and sugar for three weeks.

Skinny, small, successful.

14th April 2012 03:56:

RULES to help me:

Early nights, early mornings

Alcohol if pimms or prosecco and elderflower (otherwise just empty calories).

Plain is pure.

Nothing Mum makes.

14th April 2012 21:58

You are a disgusting human being.

You are ugly and greedy and everyone can see it.

Eating hurts everybody.

You must now have nothing to put things right to teach them all a lesson. You shouldn't eat so stop telling yourself you should. NO good comes from it. Only sadness and fat.

You don't deserve anything. You don't need anything. Get over it.

As you can see the last two notes were actually from the same day. This is a pattern that became inevitable. I would set such unrealistic goals and break them by the end of the day, finishing with a punishment of purging and some good harsh words with myself. The sequence repeated itself for most of 2012.

Some people may read this and question why I did not just make more realistic goals and stick to them and stop binging if it made me so unhappy. This is a very good point, but I couldn't help it. I considered maybe if I ate breakfast, lunch, dinner and my snacks that I might not feel the need to binge in the evening. But at the same time, every eating session was a danger zone for me. A meal was like walking a tightrope, one tiny slip and I would go crashing down into a full blown binge, purge, hate, binge, purge, hate, until I was so exhausted that I would crawl to my bed, weep and hide my shameful bulging body beneath the covers.

Truth is, I was just not ready to let go of my eating disorder. If my life being this horrendous was the only way to keep a little part of my illness, I was willing to endure it. I had become extremely attached to the thing inside of me, it was a massive part of my life and I could not bear the thought of losing it. I told my mum that recovery was like being asked to shoot my best friend. Imagine if your best friend was injured and asked you to kill them. You know you should for their benefit. But the choice to actually do it and kill them is nearly impossible.

I was not actually 'fat' throughout all of this. My weight would fluctuate depending on my frequency of binges and I remained between a BMI of 15 and 16, still a danger zone for me. It stayed like this until I discharged myself from the unit in November.

Although this was evidence that I was still very underweight, I HAD gained weight and that was all that I could see. The increasing layer of blubber which coated my once delicate frame made me sick to the stomach. Everyone assured me that I was still far too thin, but in the back of my mind I knew that I could be thinner, therefore I was fat. Any compliment containing the words 'healthy', 'well' or 'better,' immediately translated to the word 'FAT'. I could not bear it when I saw someone I had not seen in a while and they commented on how much better I looked. I had to hold myself back from punching anyone who said it. Although they were trying to encourage me, there is sometimes no worse an insult to someone with anorexia or in recovery, than telling them they look well. No one could understand the ongoing war inside my head, the depth of depression I was experiencing and the fury of the voice that constantly tortured me.

Chapter 16
CHAMPAGNE LIFESTYLE ON LEMONADE WAGES

2012 Part 2

The rest of the year continued in a similar fashion - chaotic, messy and painful. Summer was slightly better as my friends returned home from university, I was given my driving licence back and generally had more freedom and people to occupy my time.

I had discontinued my therapy with the private CBT therapist (as everyone seemed to have a problem with it and I became tired of listening to their opinions). I gave the Eating Disorders unit therapist two chances to prove to me that she was worth my time. Her voice was so quiet that I could barely hear her. I couldn't even stand two appointments and quit immediately after the first. I refused to get a new therapist as I was convinced none of them were helping, and no one at the unit wanted me to go back to the CBT guy as I was 'too attached' to him. They felt I was only seeing him for a nice chat as I enjoyed his company (party true, though I will always stand by that FACT that he was definitely helping me).

Gradually, I stopped going to my appointments at the Eating Disorders unit. I just didn't see the point. I felt like they were not helping me, they were doing the opposite by talking about numbers and calories and all the things I didn't want to hear about. On one occasion I shut my bedroom door and sat against it, as my mum frantically tried to persuade me to get in the car and go to my appointment. She rang the dietician and even held the phone to my ear as I stood there in an angry silence, refusing to open my mouth. I was becoming more aggressive as I was becoming more unhappy with myself, my life and my growing body. My state of love, peace and selflessness was disappearing at the same rate as my protruding bones. I hated that I couldn't control my outside or my inside any longer.

Alcohol consumption had increased to the point where I was drinking every day. When I saw friends, we would go to the pub or drink wine at each others houses. My new mechanism for dealing with my problems and the voices in my head was to plaster over them with alcohol. This habit confused everyone, as alcohol has such a high calorie content and I was happy to drink copious amounts of it. The difference between the calories in alcohol and food though, was that alcohol made me feel different, drunk, and helped me to forget. Food however, made me remember how fat and ugly I was and always made me feel horrible after. These alcohol infused nights usually ended in an almighty binge and purge session.

Alcohol enhances sensations, including hunger. Nothing was more attractive to me than the thought of gorging on everything in the kitchen when drunk. The best part about it was that I was so drunk I didn't care or worry about what I was eating. Purging was also easier due to the amount of drink in my system. The worst part was the following day. If you have ever had a really bad hangover, times that by ten and you have a food-over. Waking up with sick splattered pyjamas, a hugely bloated stomach that resembles an 8 month pregnant woman, excruciating head and esophagus, ulcers blistering the mouth and tongue, the most unquenchable thirst you can imagine and a churning gut. All those feelings on top of a ghastly hangover equal an extremely painful and uncomfortable day - until it hits 6pm and you still feel so awful you just repeat the cycle.

I remember nights when I came home drunk and binged and purged in the garden 'til the point of oblivion, and where my dad came and found me and had to set up a mattress at the end of his and my mum's bed for me to sleep on, because I couldn't cope with the emotions that followed. I was twenty years old and sharing my parents bedroom!

No matter how many times I was told that if I cut out drinking, the chances that binges would become less frequent was inevitable, I wouldn't listen. I knew I would still probably binge regardless, so I may as well have my escape of drinking first. I was collecting coppers and splurging them on bottles of wine, which I would secretly drink in my bedroom. The empty bottles of wine were stashed under my bed until there was no room left. I realised I had a problem when I counted around twenty bottles and that's not to mention the ones stuffed in my clothes drawers and bedside table. I think when you are drinking alone and when YOU think you are drinking too much, then you almost definitely have a problem.

I got tired of feeling so drained, bloated and hungover all the time and confessed to my parents the vague extent of my alcoholism. They already knew; I think it was fairly obvious to most of my family and friends by this stage. I couldn't go a night without a drink. Evenings were so desperately lonely and boring that the idea of wine was the only thing that would get me through them. Days where I couldn't afford to get my hands on any wine were not good days. I would sink into my own misery and be full of anger at not being able to have a drink. I would lie in bed for hours on end thinking of ways that I could get alcohol. Tears of rage would fill my livid eyes as I'd thrash around my bed, tossing and turning, completely restless.

I considered going to AA meetings to help me sort the problem. This never happened though and I carried on drinking excessively, sometimes with friends, sometimes alone. In AA you give up drink completely, which was not something I wanted to do. I wanted to give up binging and perhaps drink less, but the thought of giving up alcohol completely was a soul destroying one; what the hell would I have left in my life to enjoy.

I also began drink driving - something I never ever saw myself doing in a million years. It began when I was at a friend's house, had a few drinks but decided I wanted to go home and binge. I had consumed about half a bottle of wine, but obviously because my weight was still low, the effects it had on me were greatly increased. The urge to get back was so strong, that I got in the car and drove home, a simple journey, straight down one road. I remember feeling dazed as I drove at 50mph. I was so glad to be home so that I could get down to business, but I vowed to myself I would never drink drive again.

The second occasion I was at a pub down the same road with my best friend. We shared a bottle of wine and then had more drinks. I must have consumed over two bottles and was really drunk. Amazingly again, I made it home in one piece, though my parents could tell I had been drinking as I was slurring my words badly. They warned me never, ever to do that again, because not only was I endangering my own life, but the lives of other innocent people. They were right and I didn't do it again, until September.

My 21st birthday was fast approaching and I was feeling slightly more normal having all my friends back around me. I wanted to get a job and earn my own money. My dad was going through a difficult time with work and I became determined to gain some kind of independence, where I didn't have to live off his cash anymore.

Chapter 17
CUCUMBER SANDWICHES

My 21st birthday was was on the 4th August (like all my other birthdays), and the present from my parents was to spend a night in a French Hotel (Hotel Du Vin) in Brighton, with my best friend. The following day I was to have a 21st birthday tea party in my garden with lots of champagne, baking, friends and family surrounding me.

I drank champagne from the start to the finish of my birthday. I had an amazing time in Brighton, running hot bubble baths and drinking copious amounts of champagne at the same time. My family drove down in the evening to meet us in a glass restaurant that looked over the sea. This was the worst part of the day for me... I loved seeing and spending time with my family, but the meal itself was very unenjoyable. I think the only thing I ate was, you guessed it: asparagus - and I had to send it back as it arrived swimming in butter. After this meal my family drove home, and my best friend and I wandered the Brighton lanes drinking yet more champagne. We returned to the hotel, ran another bubble bath and went to sleep. I had an amazing day and will always remember it fondly, even if I was still ill.

The next morning we got up and went down for the pre-paid breakfast buffet. As mentioned before, breakfast is something that I just would not allow myself to have, perhaps because I know how much I would love it. The buffet looked amazing: fresh juices, any kind of cereal, pancakes, cinnamon swirls, any kind of jam you could wish for, french toast, cooked breakfasts, fruit. Buffets are a daunting entity for someone with an eating disorder to face; the sheer amount of different options available is basically terrifying. Given the opportunity, I would have devoured the entire buffet and more and then purged for days. I watched my friend pick a selection from the buffet and then order a cooked breakfast. I stuck to three consecutive mugs of black coffee, sulking to myself in silence. I looked around the grand breakfast hall at everyone smiling and indulging in their delicious pastries and jams, my mouth watered and my veins pumped pure venom around my hungry body, irritated at all these people enjoying the delicious delicacies, when it was MY birthday and I just simply couldn't.

When we got home I prepared all the treats for the 'old people's party' which I had planned, including cucumber sandwiches, scones, jams, cakes, fridge cake, oreo cake, biscuits, cookies, muffins, loaf cake. I laid them all out carefully on the kitchen table, which I had covered with an old-fashioned lace tablecloth. All my family and friends came dressed as old women and men. The effort some of them put in was astounding and I felt so grateful to everyone for coming. I drank far too much prosecco, as every time a bottle was finished, another was started. I must have had near enough eight bottles, and by the time it reached about eight o'clock, the temptation of the divine tea party I had made for everyone else, got all too much. I had had nothing, as I watched everyone else excitedly experimenting with each delicious treat. I had subconsciously surrounded myself with the perfect binge feast, but because there were so many people there I had no opportunity to go wild. I found myself sneaking in and out of the kitchen pretending to 'get something' or pretending to go to the toilet. I was in actual fact shoving cucumber sandwiches up my sleeves, cakes in my pockets, biscuits in my mouth - running in and out of the toilet, flushing it continuously to cover up the sound of me munching on whatever I could steal without anyone seeing. I was so drunk I would not be surprised if all my friends and family noticed, but I put this thought to the back of my mind, as it was too humiliating for me to contemplate. Slowly but surely the guests departed and I didn't even notice. I was so wrapped up in my secret binge mission. I only noticed much later when no one was there, and still I continued my frantic feast. It was MY birthday after all, why should everyone except me get to eat all these cakes.

I ended my 21st birthday with my head down the toilet and my hand down my throat, emptying my insides out over the bathroom, black makeup staining my red eyes and puffy face. I slumped on the sick splattered floor and looked around at the mess of regurgitated sandwiches and cakes around me. My knuckles were bloody and my stomach, painful and swollen. Happy fucking birthday to me I thought, before dragging my sorry self to bed, full of shame and disgust.

The following day I had my interview at Monsoon, the perfect starting job for me as it was just a ten minute drive from my house and only for weekend shifts. I was still drunk, or very hungover, but I managed to do ok and got myself the job. I started the following week and it was the biggest step I had taken in my recovery. I found it extremely tiring, as I was not used to being on my feet for long hours. I also got a lot of over-time which included working from 9 until 6.

I made the decision not to tell work about my illness. Pretty much everyone who knew me, vaguely knew what happened to me. My friends, family and fellow University students saw it happen, my Uni informed everyone why I had left, those who supported me through it confided in others, and people could just see anyway. Since being diagnosed I have always been very open in talking about what happened to me, partly because everyone already knew and partly because it was real, it happened, and I can't change that. It was very difficult to keep what felt like one of the most imperative times of my life a secret. I would find myself spilling out information to people more frequently than I would have liked. Though I am not my illness, the way in which it turned my life upside down has shaped me as a person and is a huge part of me. It is difficult to hide, and revealing it almost offers an explanation for my sometimes intense mannerisms and mind set; it made me the way I was.

By not telling work about my illness, it took away my ability and freedom to make excuses (something that I was very good at). When feeling faint or tired, sick or hungover, I just got on with it, because to them I had no reason to be feeling like that every day. When I walked into work, it was the only place in which I could not be 'Ill Lydia', I had to be 'Normal Lydia'. At first it was very difficult to keep this big secret to myself, especially when feeling weak, or when conversations of diet arose. Being asked to go up and down the stairs ten times in a shift to the stock room would make me feel dizzy as my body was still very fragile when I started. There were occasions when I wanted to turn around and scream, 'YES I DO MIND GOING DOWN AGAIN. I AM SICK, YOU ARE NOT, YOU GO PLEASE!', but I didn't, I held my tongue, gritted my teeth and got on with it as best I could.

Though it was a massive challenge to hide that whole part of myself, pretend to be normal, ignore my anxieties when I caught a glimpse of my 'huge' frame in one of the many mirrors at work, or just hold my tongue when I wanted to shout out so bad that I was feeling awful, I think it was really good for me.

When everyone surrounding you is aware of the struggles which you endure on a daily basis and the near death state you were in not so long ago, it is difficult for them to treat you as they would everyone else. My parents and friends worried about me a lot, and I was lucky enough that they had the understanding and I had the freedom to tell them whatever I wanted, whenever I wanted. If I was to refuse to eat and name an obscure fruit from a non-existent Island on the other side of the globe, I have no doubt that my mum or dad would have found a way to get it to me. That is their dedication, how loving they are, how sick they knew I was, and how privileged I was.

Chapter 18
DOROTHY, MY GUARDIAN ANGEL

From August onwards I worked every opportunity I could. I felt useful, grown up, and had to force myself, to avoid depression and anxiety. Smiling and being friendly to every single customer who walked into the shop, when inside you are all over the place, have absolutely no confidence, are a complete mess, hurting and dark, is not fucking easy. Some days I wanted to be dead, some days I just wanted to hide away and cry. I had to learn to face up to acting my age again, which was a traumatising step in the right direction.

I felt proud of myself for doing it despite how difficult I found it at first. I enjoyed having my own money (even though I swapped most of it for wine), my own separate place and occupation, which did not involve my family, my friends, or even Ana.

Although things appeared smoother on the outside than they had been previously, I was still tearing myself apart inside. The next big commotion in my life was extremely dramatic. I had been drinking wine at my friends house. I had driven myself there and the plan was for me to stay the night. As we spoke and laughed in her kitchen together into the late hours of the night, I became increasingly drunk. It was one of those situations where I was drinking for the sake of it, every time my glass became empty, I felt empty too, so I would top it up constantly. Molly liked a glass of wine too, but the difference was that she could enjoy just one glass slowly and feel content. As it got later, I got drunk, my appetite increased and I could feel a binge coming on. Generally speaking my binges only usually happened in the privacy and safety of my own home and there are only a handful of occasions where they have taken place either in other people's houses, or in public - on a train for instance. Once Molly went to bed, I could not stop eating. I bought myself some food from the corner shop which I had walked to once everyone was asleep, but as soon as everything was gone, I needed more. I ended up eating a stupid amount of food out of Molly's family kitchen and am still so ashamed of myself to this day. When the episode was over and I came round, I felt so humiliated about what I had just done and incredibly guilty for taking what wasn't mine, that I needed to get out. I could not be sick in her house; she had a little brother asleep upstairs and it felt so wrong and disrespectful, even though I had already lost all morals and created a huge mess in their kitchen and eaten their weekly shopping. In a state of complete humiliation, shock and dread about the consequences of my behaviour, I decided I had no option but to get the hell out of there and drive home.

As mentioned earlier, I had driven under the influence of alcohol on two previous occasions, where both times I was very lucky and nothing happened. This time however, I was in such a state at myself (I couldn't believe what I had just done) and had drunk around two bottles of wine, that I wasn't so lucky. I snuck out of her house without so much as a sound, quietly got into the car and drove out of the driveway. From hers, my house is about a twenty-five minute drive away and the route consists of lots of winding country lanes. I can't remember the drive, but I'm almost certain I was definitely going too fast. There are so many different things to concentrate on when driving, speed, mirrors, positioning, gears, lights, etc, but all I could think about was the contents of my stomach, shocked at myself for eating all of Molly's family's food, and ashamed to be me. As I sped along the country road completely oblivious to how terribly and carelessly I was driving, I could barely see the road. I don't even know if the lights were on. My eyes were hazed over and the only thing that I could see was the purge at the end of the tunnel. I was nearly home and swung round the bend of the dark country lane. I remember suddenly feeling like I was going way too fast, I felt a little out of control, then I felt completely out of control. I attempted to slam on the breaks when it hit me how fast I was going, and I don't know exactly what happened next, but I can guess I hit the accelerator instead of the break. There was a heavy thud that vibrated right through me as the left wheel hit the bank along the side of the narrow road. Next thing I knew, I was flying through the sky and my mind was screaming, "THIS IS IT THEN. THIS IS IT." It happened scarily quickly. Spinning through the air upside down in a car was the craziest feeling, adrenaline pumped through my body and thoughts pierced my head. This changed in a matter of split seconds when the car came crashing down, upside down on the road. I heard an almighty smash of the car landing and the glass shattering into a million shards. I woke up upside down in pitch-black silence. The first thought that came to my head was that I needed to get out of the car in case it exploded. I used my arm to smash away the remaining glass from the window and crawled out. I could not believe what had just happened and was in complete shock. I ran away from the car, screaming for my mum and dad. I was a good half an hour's walk down dangerous country lanes from my house, but was too scared to re-enter the car to try and find my phone incase of a fire or something else hitting it. I started jogging in the direction of home in the darkness. The only sound was my screams for help, but no one answered. Tears flooded across my cold, shocked face as I ran as fast as I could, struggling to breathe and crying out for help the entire way, heart pumping shock around my body. There was no one to hear my cries though, I was alone and anything could have happened. As if that was not dangerous enough, I then proceeded to flag down the first car that passed. A man stopped and I climbed into the back of his car, scared, confused and desperate. Luckily he was not a serial killer and drove me home, where I got out and screamed for my parents once more until they heard me from their bedroom window, ran downstairs and opened the door.

I believe that night something saved me. The fact that I wasn't dead was a miracle in itself, but I was completely uninjured, apart from a scratch on my arm. To this day, I still cannot comprehend how on earth it could be physically possible for me to not only survive that, but to come out with not even a trace of damage. The only explanation that it could be, was that something shielded me from the danger, took the danger and the pain for me and guided me, protecting me from any real physical harm. My mum told me that the angel looking over me was my grandmother, and I know she was there with me. It is only when such impossible miracles happen that I know there is a higher power; I am reminded that something up there must have wanted me to survive all of this.

Once home my parents had no choice but to call the police as the car was left in the middle of a country lane which could be very dangerous for other drivers. An ambulance was sent to the house to take me into hospital to get checked over. The fact that I had been knocked unconscious in the car indicated that there may be some form of damage. I rubbed my lips around a wine glass before the ambulance arrived, and poured some wine over the glass and the table. My alibi was that I had run home and was far too afraid to tell my parents that I had smashed up their car, so I drank in the kitchen before they found me.

I was breathalysed in the ambulance on the way to hospital and failed miserably. The paramedics could not quite understand how I was way over the limit if I had only just started drinking when I got home. It was clear to them that I was telling a lie... but I couldn't risk losing my license, or getting a criminal record or anything else. My persona was already tainted through my medical records; I desperately did not want a criminal one to add to the list of my fuck ups.

I spent the night in hospital with my mum and two police officers. They questioned and grilled me about my story, trying to cause a slip up. It didn't work and I just wanted to go home. They then told me that they had called out a forensic doctor who would take my bloods and they would be able to see from the sample exactly how much I drank, as well as exactly WHEN I drank it. I thought, 'shit, this is it', and I would be in even more trouble now for lying. But in the back of my mind something assured me that they must have been talking bullshit, so I said fine and stuck to my story.

I was arrested in the hospital, but released once my bloods had been taken at five in the morning because the results could take six weeks to come back. I was terrified of the consequences of my actions. Usually I could make stupid mistakes and end up dodging the outcomes if I didn't like them, but I knew that there was no way out this time.

Two weeks later I got a phone call from the police. They informed me that my bloods had returned and showed that I was not over the limit. I couldn't believe my ears... I even asked if he was sure? I was one hundred percent way over the limit and should certainly have been banned from driving, or at least punished in SOME way. He said there was no mistake and they were not going to be taking the case any further. I cannot believe how lucky I was to get away with that, with not even a scrape, let alone a ban. I had a lawyer lined up and everything. The only logical explanation as to why I got off scotch free was that they must have messed up the procedure, the bloods, or lost them..

The relevance of this incident within my story is not the accident itself, but more the reactions. Ask anyone who has been in a severe car accident how they felt after and they will tell you that they were completely shaken up. You're supposed to be shaken up after something like that happening to you. Fear of the damage that could have been done to yourself and other people, scared of death, guilty for breaking the law, nervous to get back behind a wheel, repelling alcohol for what it had caused and sorry to your parents for writing off their car.

Surprise, surprise, I felt nothing. I tried to make myself have nightmares about the accident and fool myself into having flashbacks, but the truth is, none of that happened and I wasn't even sure if the car accident was something I had imagined. It wasn't and my parents will tell anyone that. It was yet another horrible experience for them to deal with, because of my illness. They were shocked, upset, no, distraught, but mostly grateful that I was still alive. The only thing that was on my mind the following morning was the brioche I had stolen from my friends the night before, the food piled up in my stomach, pushing against my sides and making me fatter and fatter. The obvious one to point the finger at for this accident would be myself and alcohol. However the cause of the entire incident was once again down to my eating disorder. The mindset caused me to drink to escape my thoughts, the bulimia caused me to binge and steal, the 'me' caused me to feel humiliated and disgusted and the bulimia caused me to get behind the wheel due to the overpowering need and urge to purge as soon as I could.

I am not a bad person or a lawbreaker. In this case I have to know that driving under the influence is something I would never in a millions years do, if I did not have the illness. Perhaps that is why the danger of the car crash has never properly registered; it was not me driving that car, it was the eating disorder that I was possessed by.

The next day I had a few glasses of wine and a few weeks later, was back behind the wheel when we got a new car, as if it never even happened.

Chapter 19
I WILL BE BRAVE / I'LL LOVE YOU FROM AFAR

My friends were freaked out by what had happened in the car accident. They were also very upset watching me self-destruct. They had seen me way before Ana had gouged her claws deep into my skin and dragged me in to her dark world. They found it excruciatingly painful to hear me express my desire to lose weight again, to say I missed my bones, to tell them how I was feeling. The problem here though is that if I could not express my true feelings to my best ever friends in the world, then surely I would become even more lonely, depressed and more likely to hurt myself.

Libby became more distant. Jo and Nat had been acting strangely with me for a while too, which I did think was very odd. Nat and I had spent pretty much every second at home together for several years. We became extremely close and were always in contact. So, one day when she said she was going over to Jo's and I asked if I could come too, she said, "No, it's probably best if you don't." I was extremely surprised. Neither of them would reply to my texts and I genuinely had no idea what I had done wrong. This sent me into a flurry of thoughts and questions to myself about what I had done to upset them? Had I said something? Had I been mean? I literally couldn't understand where this had come from and why no one would tell me what was wrong. I felt more alone than ever that day.

Jo and I had been friends all through school. We had been through many ups and downs throughout our friendship, but always managed to turn it around and end up closer and stronger than before. When first experiencing bulimia, I spent a lot of time at Jo's house. My sister found the purging extremely difficult to deal with and my parents were becoming increasingly frustrated at me for not attending day care. This caused so much tension in our household that I went over to Jo's and stayed there whenever I could. She was more than happy to have me there and we would talk for hours about both of our problems. When I went home the next day she would ask me to return again that night, and I would.

Anyway, one Sunday I had work all day. I had not eaten a thing and was so tired. Libby and Jo had contacted me and asked to meet me in a pub for a drink when I finished work. I was overjoyed that they were going to come and see me and felt excited all day, counting down the minutes until I finished my shift. Once work was over, I walked to where we were supposed to meet, but no one was there. After an hour of waiting in the freezing cold on my own, I rang them. They said they were only just leaving and would be there soon (a forty minute walk - so I knew they wouldn't). I was quite annoyed as I could have gone home and got something to eat within that time... but I ended up pretending it was fine and went to sit in the pub alone, waiting for them for another hour.

When they arrived I was so happy to see them, but I got an instant vibe that something was not right. As Libby went to the bar to order the drinks, Jo and I sat there awkwardly. She asked me how work was and all those normal questions and I bluntly asked her what was up and if I had done something wrong. She smiled awkwardly, and quite condescendingly replied, "let's just wait for Libby to get back yeah?" I felt confused and very uneasy about her response and how she said it.

Obviously this meant I had done something wrong, so I sat there in silence feeling extremely uncomfortable and anxious. When Libby returned to the table I asked them straight out what I had done and what was going on. Slowly but surely they managed to explain that they couldn't really cope with hearing me speak about how I am feeling anymore, as it was too depressing for them to hear and it was upsetting them; I was too depressing. They said it was the hardest conversation they have ever had to have and had been losing sleep over it. I was completely and utterly shocked, firstly that they had been talking about this for some time amongst themselves, and secondly, that they had left me completely in the dark about it until inviting

173

me to a pub for drinks after a long and exhausting day at work, to express their feelings to me in public.

I was completely humiliated - that I had been so excited to see them all day, and that I had been opening up my heart to those friends, telling them every dark feeling I was having or experiencing, because they had told me they were always there for me and that I could tell them anything... only to find out that they had all been discussing how I am too depressing and concocting how to tell me that I am too depressing. I couldn't believe it. It felt like three breakups all in one go. Jo said she did not mind seeing me, but it would be better if it were once in a while and I could not really stay over anymore. I felt like I was being attacked. The longest I had ever stayed at her house was two consecutive nights and only because she had asked me to come back after the first.

Shaking with a silent humiliation and trying to swallow back the lump of sadness that had formed in my throat, I excused myself to smoke a cigarette. I sat alone and thought to myself, how fucking dare they get me excited all day for going out and getting to see them, making me wait an hour in the cold, only to fucking ambush me like this. I was so angry that they hadn't come to me and said how they felt individually, rather than joining forces and tricking me into going out for a drink. Nat wasn't even there as she was away with her boyfriend, but Jo and Libby assured me that she was a part of their allied force. They had ALL been talking about me.

Once back inside they pleaded with me to say something, as I just sat at the table trying to fight back tears in silence. I told them that I had nothing to say which caused a terrible atmosphere. I genuinely didn't though. If they were asking me to stop telling them how I feel because they found it too depressing to listen to, how was I meant to say anything now? I ended up replying, "sorry, of course I'm depressing. I've got severe depression". I then called my dad to come and pick me up, as I couldn't bear to accept a ride home from Libby or Jo, even though they followed me down the street begging me to. I felt completely betrayed and more alone than ever. When I got into my dad's car, he asked me what was wrong and I burst into tears. I went straight to my room when I got home, unable to eat or face anyone, I lay under my duvet crying for the next few hours until I was able to sleep.

That evening marks the end of an era of friendship for me. I have forgiven them all. I can see where they were coming from now, I just think they went about it in the completely wrong way. They did what they felt they had to do at the time I suppose and I respect that, but none of our friendships would ever be the same as they were before, and I have cried many times over this. We grew up like sisters and always had such a strong connection which I believed was impossible to break. I felt such great loss that day and for the following years where they (who had been my best friends for so many years), were no longer in my life.

Since the whole fiasco, Nat and I have reconnected. It was easier to do this with her as she wasn't there on the night and she was the first to reach out to me. We never really spoke about what happened, we just managed to pick up our friendship where we left off and went back to normal, which I was so happy about, as was she. Moving forward is much better than looking back. I never spoke with Jo again after that evening, and to this day (6 years on), I still haven't. I think it was such a loss of what was and could still be, a great friendship, but I also know I won't get that back. The binding between us was severed beyond repair that night.

Recently Libby and I went away for a weekend together, almost six years after this night. We laughed uncontrollably and somehow were exactly the same as we used to be. It was amazing to see her as I had dreamt many times of what it would be like now - whether we would still be the same, and have anything in common anymore. She sent me a very touching letter apologising for what happened all those years ago and of course I replied saying not to apologise, because I forgave her the same day. We are in touch now and I feel so lucky that we were able to keep our bond somewhere or somehow, even without speaking for so long. We grew up together and the majority of my school and growing up memories are with her. Sadly because of what happened, we have missed out on a lot of each others lives and have ventured down different paths where we have seen and experienced very different things. It is hard to catch up on such a long period of time where so much has happened, but even so, I was very glad to see her.

If this illness has taught me one thing, it is that honesty is most definitely the best policy. I had every tiny bit of privacy confiscated from me and had to adjust to to being watched constantly, violated both physically and mentally. The prodding of needles into my every vein to extract my blood which I did not offer, the digging around my head for answers, the weekly documentation of my weight, heartbeat, feelings, thoughts and mood. When put in such a position there comes a time when there is no point in hiding anything; you may as well walk around naked shouting your most private secrets through a megaphone.

It's strange to think about really. I used to be the most secretive person I knew. I kept things to myself, I was embarrassed extremely easily, and quite liked the element of mystery that my character portrayed. To go from that to an open book of big blatant letters and words projecting out of me for all to see and read, is such a contradiction. It is as if through my self-destructive illness I lost all self-respect, self-control and morals towards myself. I used to care so much about what people thought of me, and though I am still very self-conscious in some ways, it is more my own opinion of myself that matters, as I know everyone who loves me excuses my barbaric behaviours and understands that they happened because I was ill.

Sometimes I find words spilling out of my mouth regarding very personal occurrences, ones that I would really wish to keep to myself, but I cannot help but spew out this information before I realise that in fact it is pretty private. Once said, I cannot take these things back, and the more I let out, the less privacy I have, and the less shame I feel. As time has passed and since my illness, I have become more and more open and believe it is one of the things that has helped me the most to recover. Not having to feel unbearable shame about myself lifts a huge weight off my shoulders, and the kind reactions of others surprised me and encouraged me to continue sharing.

Chapter 20
I TOOK THE RED PILL

I began seeing a new therapist in the autumn. Because I had seen such a number of different people already and had stuck with none, I was very reluctant to start all over again. I was binging and purging a lot, but I was also working a lot, so believed that I was fairly in control, I was fine as I was, plodding along. All of my family urged me to give this new guy a shot, as they believed it could be the answer to the question of how I was going to recover.

'Cognitive Hypnotherapist' was the new guy's title. I was intrigued at the idea of hypnosis, but went along to the first appointment on Harley Street with no intention of letting him in, or letting him change me, but just to see what it was all about... I found him completely intriguing and I thoroughly enjoyed our appointments in which we discussed perceptions of reality, the wiring of the brain and the fact that I am Auditory Digital. I found the whole personality type thing fascinating. It gave me an understanding of why I think in the way that I do and why certain things appear or seem different to me than they do to a lot of other people.

Auditory Digital comes from a science-based practise called Neuro-Linguistic Programming (NLP), which is used as a tool to understand the brain and the way we think and why we behave like we do. There are four types; Visual, Auditory, Kinaesthetic and Auditory Digital. The first three are fairly self-explanatory, in that people interpret things through one dominant sense - sight, sound or touch. Auditory Digital processing however, is about the words and specific language we use to describe things. AD's are more disconnected from senses and it is the meanings of words that are processed by the brain, rather than the sounds.

Learning about these different ways of thinking taught me a lot about myself and helped to explain why I saw things in such a different way to other people. Travis and the way he spoke completely absorbed me.

I wrote a blog on the film, 'The Matrix', as that film made so much sense to me..

January 11th 2013 06:24:

The red pill and it's opposite the blue pill are pop culture symbols representing the choice between the blissful ignorance of illusion (blue) and embracing the sometimes painful truth of reality (red).

The matrix is an unreal film. I usually hate films, but I related to this one so well.

I think too much. Constantly. I don't know what silence really sounds like, apart from when I have JUST woken up at 6am and for a few moments while I smoke a cigarette, I hear nothing. Then, mid cigarette the birds pipe up, the thoughts start questioning. They continue until I manage to fall asleep at night. I get very confused. All I know about myself is some of the highs I felt last year, which were very, very high, then the pain of the lows. Real, raw pain. I remember the buzz and I remember the agony. But before then I cannot remember who I was or who I wanted to be. I wonder often how other people know who they are. How they get up and get on with their daily routine, no questions. How they relax. How they do certain things without questioning or agonising over them. How they just know who they are and how they act. How their behaviours and thoughts are so set and they believe and know a certain something. It's as if everyone knows something, some great secret of how to live life normally, but I was never told. I feel confused how people complete things and then get a job, then married, then children, then retire. How do they know what to do or how to get there?

I'm trying to work myself out. I definitely took the red pill.

"Everything is an illusion and nothing is real" is my favourite lyric taken from Van Morrison's 'Enlightenment'. I don't think I am enlightened of course, far from it... I do however think I see things differently from the norm. My personality type is auditory digital. People of this type often have a constant conversation going on with themselves. Attempting to find meaning and reason within things.

Apparently a good 80 percent of the population took the blue pill. They live in ignorant bliss. They do what we are supposed to do. School-Uni-gapyah-job-money-house-partner-reproduce-et c etc... To me this seems somewhat boring. What's the point if it's boring. I want to understand what we are and why we are here.

Blue pill people tend not to question their reality, as they are quite content living like they do and like everyone else does. But that other 20 percent of red pill people have an understanding that EVERYTHING is an illusion. No one really knows who they are. Each day we wake up and create who we are, we create our day, we make our story. I don't believe that anything is real anymore, and I think that is why I'm absolutely content with sharing these

words as I may come across crazy to the blues, but nothing
is real anyway so I don't mind.

Travis was my Morpheus and I was Neo. I saw him as someone who could lead me out of my eating disorders, should I let him. The problem arose when he went to hypnotise me though. Anorexia sufferers like to be in control of themselves, things have to be the way they like them, special orders, routines and rituals. The idea of handing over all my self-control to Travis and not knowing how he could change the wiring of my brain was too scary. I wanted to do it, but I did not want to let someone else have all my control. What if I lost my eating disorder completely? What if I didn't care at all about food or weight or other people's opinions and became obese and obsessed with McDonalds? He assured me that this would not happen and this was not his aim, but I couldn't trust that he knew exactly what would happen. I wasn't ready to sacrifice my eating disorder all together. I was still holding on to what was still there as tightly as I could. Travis could distinguish which part of me was talking to him and when, much of which was Anorexia and not Lydia.

The decision to recover is a difficult one. Obviously the idea of not having all this shit on my mind 24/7 was extremely appealing and in a way I would have loved nothing more than to be normal again. At the same time, my ED had become a huge part of my identity; it had altered my personality traits and shaped me into the person that I am to this day. To let go completely of such a traumatic part of my life was a massive ask and to be honest, I wasn't really ready then. I didn't want what I had been through to be forgotten by myself or anyone else. My illness gave me an explanation for my behaviours and without it I feared I would be less easily excused when I messed up (which was frequently) and less sympathised with. It had become my crutch to hold me up and I wasn't sure how I would be were it completely erased from my life. I was scared of change.

Though I enjoyed his sessions, I wasn't letting Travis progress with his treatment and actually hypnotise me. Each session was around two hundred pounds and I knew deep down I was never going to let him do his work. It was for this reason that I decided to terminate my therapy and start looking for yet another solution.

Chapter 21
LIVE ALOHA

It was around Christmas 2012 and I felt so different than I had done the previous year. The glitter seemed dull, the lights were not so bright, the excitement was half hearted and I was really looking forward to it being over to be honest. I was completely out of control with my eating and knew that this day of food was going to be one of the biggest struggles I had faced all year. I love the smell of Christmas food and could remember how amazing the parsnips were the previous year. What didn't help is that we had Christmas at home and home is the place where I lost control the most. I feel on edge, yet too comfortable there. It is my habitat and it's as if no one sees me when I am behind the closed door of my house. I turn into some kind of wild animal, all emotions are let loose, all inhibitions are lost. I cannot walk into the kitchen at home without considering a binge. I cannot walk into the bathroom after eating without considering a purge.

I drank too much champagne (yet again) before Christmas lunch was served. I can't say I even remember it, but I know I ate way too much and remember sneaking in and out of the kitchen long into the afternoon, then in and out of the bathroom trying to rid myself of the food I had not deserved. I hated that day and felt selfishly envious once again of everyone else's enjoyment. I was surrounded by all my triggers and I was unable to see past them to the meaning of the day or my family. I spent the entire day consumed by thoughts of food and then consuming food.

New years eve was also very different from the previous year. It was cold, dark and pouring with rain; my mood was similar to that of the weather. I felt ill and went out and drank for less than an hour before calling my brother to come and collect me. 2012 ended as 2013 started... My head down the toilet, purging into the New Year after attempting to fill the empty void inside myself with a final almighty binge. I wept into my pillow as the clock struck twelve, lonely, hurting and completely miserable. I couldn't believe I had ended and started a year like this, and I was pretty devastated.

January and February came and went with nothing of particular interest happening. Binge, purge, work, repeat. Through all of the binging my body was starting to return back to its normal shape and I was distraught. I cried in the shower, grabbing at my thighs and punching myself in the stomach, frustrated and angry at what had happened to the body I almost killed myself for. I was starting to look more normal, no one was telling me my legs were too skinny anymore, no one was asking me to eat more, no one was NOTICING me.

It was on an all day shift at work that I felt something, something I hadn't felt in a long, long time and something that I did not like. I had known for a while that this day coming was possible.. and here it was. I rushed to the toilet and saw that terrifying red stain for the first time in over two years and I didn't have a clue what to do. It was like being sixteen and starting my period for the first time all over again. I had forgotten what it felt like and my heart sank. To me this meant that I was no longer ill. The absence of menstruation is a clear indicator that your body is malnourished. When you're body is so weak, it will stop releasing eggs as it is not strong enough to carry or support a child, nor do you have enough energy to even release eggs to be fertilised. My fertility being at a standstill was the last physical symptom of anorexia that I felt I still had for sure, so when it returned, I was completely horrified. I stood in the toilet at work holding back tears and shaking with fear, not knowing what to do. Why was this happening to me? I hadn't missed these monthly inconveniences at all, quite the opposite; it was the best symptom ever: no nonsense, and a clear reminder to myself that I was still thin.

There was nothing I could do, I had to go back to the shop floor with toilet roll stuffed in my knickers and continue to work for another four hours without bursting into tears. Once home, I crawled under my duvet and hid there, away from the world, away from anyone.

People who genuinely want to fully recover and are trying to do so with all their might would probably take this event as an achievement. I took it as a curse from above, and couldn't get my head around the fact that my body was at a healthy enough weight to do this. It was horrible.

Whenever I worked full days I avoided food like the plague. I couldn't bear the thought of eating on my lunch break and having to go back to standing in the shop for another four hours, unable to purge, feeling full and disgusting. I also still couldn't really bring myself to eat in public. Once home I would stuff myself with a huge salad and the routine continued.

Since my diagnosis I had fantasised about going away, getting out of England and more importantly getting out of my head. I strongly believed that I needed to see and experience other parts of the world in order to want to truly recover. I needed to see something other than the dull walls of my bedroom day in, day out, the shop I worked in, or the toilet bowl. It was a bit of a catch-22 situation. I needed to get better in order to go away, but I thought I needed to go away to be able to get better. I saved up some money and booked a flight out to Hawaii in February 2013.

Hawaii is a spiritual island, miles away from anywhere. I was invited to stay with my dad's friend who I had only met twice, before flying across the world by myself. She invited me and meant it, so I jumped at the opportunity as deep down I really felt like it was something that I needed to do.

The journey there took a very long time, ten and a half hours to Washington, then twelve hours on to Honolulu. Between frantically worrying about what my larger body was going to look like in a bikini and wondering what I was going to eat, I somehow managed to sleep pretty much the entire journey. Upon arrival, we went out to dinner then back to the beautiful apartment. It was clean, bright and had an incredible window that looked right out over the ocean below us. In my bed at night I could hear the movement of the waves, crashing against the wall just beneath me. This sound soothed me to sleep each night like nothing ever had, and I've never felt more relaxed as I did lying there, listening to that sound. For once I was not craving a glass of wine to unwind or relax before sleep. I was embracing the incredible sounds, smells and beauty of nature.

I met such a variety of different people on my trip, many who told me stories that taught me things about myself. I was unable to purge and managed to eat more than usual as I needed energy for all the walking we did.

The food out there was so fresh, with many vegan options that I felt quite comfortable trying. I did gain a little weight in Hawaii and I knew it, but for a short while I was more ok with this than I had ever been. I was in the most beautiful place on earth and I tried very hard not to let my self-loathing or disordered eating ruin this wonderful experience.

From around this time the previous year, with the depression, binge, purge, weight gain etc... I haven't fully explained that I wasn't really trying to recover any longer. I missed the gap between my thighs, the way people would stare at me as I strutted on my skeletal legs down the street, arms swinging like wishbones, dangling from my sharp shoulders. I missed the buzz and the high from starvation, the hollow feeling of emptiness, and the sensation of being in a different world which I found deep within anorexia. All my clothes looked different on me, tighter, more fitted, more uncomfortable. As a fashion lover, I knew how I wanted my clothes to look and to me they didn't look right at all.

I returned from Hawaii and my mum told me she couldn't remember seeing me looking so relaxed. The energy from the Island had obviously reached me and the Vitamin D from the sun had done my mood the world of good. I had pushed myself out of my comfort zone and seen new and exciting things, which in turn healed me inside and helped to draw positivity from my situation. I fell in love with the island and am sure I will go back as soon as I can. It is a place of peace, calm and healing which played an extremely special part in my recovery.

After being back from Hawaii for a few weeks, I slowly reverted back to my chaotic routine. The binging and purging was again increasingly frequent and my desperation to lose weight was causing the opposite effect. The more I seemed to think about not eating, or not binging, the more I ate and binged and purged. It was so frustrating and annoying to know that you were amazing at losing weight, you did it so well and it was your one talent... to then lose the ability completely. Every time I would eat less for a day, a few days later all hell would break loose and I would go on some manic escapade to see just how much I could eat this time. My hate for my body grew and grew as my self-esteem shrank away.

Chapter 22
METAPHORICAL EMPTY SUITCASE

In April I agreed to start seeing a new therapist. It was clear that I had not recovered as much mentally as I had thought. The problems of bulimia and alcoholism were continuing to intensify, making my life extremely miserable and difficult.

My dad contacted a friend who practises Psychotherapy, who recommended someone for me to see in London. I was reluctant to attend again as it meant starting all over, telling my story from the very beginning again, explaining four years of my life all, over, again.

To my surprise I was happy with seeing this woman. All of my previous therapist and counsellors had been men.

We delved deep into potential reasons for my illness and behaviours, as well as discovering patterns that the behaviours followed. I saw Rita twice a week in Covent Garden and the routine that this gave to my life was important. I always saw her on the same days, at the same time, and this alone was extremely helpful to me in breaking up my boring week, giving me some kind of structure and making feel like I was actively going somewhere in my life, rather than spending my time locked in the house thinking about food, drinking, binging, purging, then crying, every single day.

Together we investigated elements of my childhood which could have played a role in triggering the disease. Although I found some of the conversations and observations she had, extremely bizarre - like when she told me my favourite restaurant was Wagamama because it has the word 'mamma' in it, which indicated I was looking for nurture from my Mother?.. Or when she asked me whether I was breast fed or not as that could have played a role. I stuck with it however, and tried to use the sessions as best I could. The fact that I am the middle child, sandwiched between two talented siblings, came up frequently in sessions. I have so much love and respect for my brother and sister; they are my best friends. I always admired them both so much and wished to have things that they had, or to be more like them.

I know that relationships with siblings are a commonly known factor in contributing to the development of anorexia. Competing for attention, as well as achievements against such talented siblings perhaps stayed inside me, and caused me to feel less worthy of nurture than them. I think I felt that I didn't matter as much as they did; they were more important and I just happened to be there attempting to fit in where I could.

For a big part of my life I somehow saw my family in sections. My mum and sister were one unit, slender, lean, beautiful; my dad and brother were another unit, well built, strong and tall. The final unit was me, alone, and I never quite knew where I fitted into the equation that I had created. I was not thin, nor pretty like I saw my mum and sister to be; I thought I was more chunky and built like my brother and dad. I remember feeling so jealous when my mum would complain about her legs being too skinny, and how I would feel angry when my sister hated being tall and slim. I was forever examining the stretch marks on my thighs, the flab on my chest (boobs), the expanding hips and curves forming as I was becoming a woman. For as long as I can remember I have always been unhappy with my body. As a child I remember wearing leotards at ballet and asking why my tummy stuck out and my friend's didn't. She was tiny and I felt like a giant next to her. I felt as though I took up too much space.

There is one specific photograph taken on a family holiday in France that sends shivers through my spine and makes me flush red with embarrassment at myself whenever I see it. In the photo I am sitting on a bench in a bikini top and skirt with my mum and sister beside me. They are both tanned and slim and looking effortlessly good; next to them is me, ghostly pale, probably double the width and sucking my stomach in with all my might. That photo haunts me and I remember how disgusted I felt when I first saw it.

It's so difficult to try and come up with reasons as to why an eating disorder develops. Environmental, social and cultural factors all play a huge role definitely. There has been much research into the idea that eating disorders are hereditary, or that some people are just born with a certain defect in their brain; they have the switch that once clicked will trigger anorexia or bulimia at some stage in their life. I could sit here all day and pick apart my childhood, remember comments people once said to me that didn't make me feel good, but to tell the truth that isn't what is going to help me. To me, my childhood couldn't have been any better than it was; I know how lucky I have been and will always be eternally grateful for that.

Not eating at first, became a way of me controlling myself and then the reactions of those around me. It was all pretty subconscious, but when I think about it now I realise how I used what I put in my body as a way to show that no one could tell me what to do, no one could affect me, no one could control me. When angry or bitter with my mum as my illness was developing, I remember the easy option was to not eat, that would really show them, and there was nothing they could do about it. It was the only thing that was mine, my decision. If my mum made me food, I wouldn't eat it because I wanted to be as thin as she was.

It's a similar situation with bulimia, in that I can now identify patterns. An example would be that when no one was home to greet me I felt angry, alone or bored, this easily led me to subconsciously become possessed by the desire to binge, to fill a void, to make myself feel less alone, less bored. I'd take my anger out on food and on myself for feeling the way I did. I became so blinded by the disorder and the desire that I genuinely had no control over my behaviour.

I attempted suicide on numerous occasions in this state of mind. Trying to purge and not being able to was possibly the most frustrating and torturous experience. Sometimes I got so annoyed with my stupid body and damaged gag reflex that I would feel the need to punish it as much as possible because it had let me down and I'd be stuck with food inside me. I once drank a cleaning product in an attempt to induce vomiting (didn't work). I have overdosed three times - partly in an attempt to make myself sick, partly because I felt so bad about my actions that I actually wanted to die. I have bitten and scratched myself, tried to suffocate myself and even driven my car on the roof.

I remember one evening when my brother and his girlfriend returned to find me in my bedroom with my dressing gown cord tied around my neck, trying to hang myself from my bed frame. I felt so desperate, distraught and alone. My thoughts were going wild and no matter how hard I tried, my body was just too exhausted to bring all the food back up. I went into my room, pulled down the blind so that I was in darkness and selected a playlist consisting of all my favourite songs. I felt limp, my mind free, my soul separate, allowing me to escape the nightmare that I was completely trapped in.

I closed my eyes and listened to the lyrics of the songs as the darkness and lack of oxygen soothed my frantic mind into submission. It was the only way I could think of to reach the state of peace and calm that I craved so badly, to kill that thing inside of me. My brother and his girlfriend found me, head dangling, still awake, but peaceful. He ripped the cord from around my neck, grabbed me in his arms and put me on my bed. They comforted me and looked after me for the rest of the evening. It must have been very shocking for them to see and the next day my parents were in tears upon hearing of what I had tried to do. I was however, completely unphased, no big deal.

I always tell myself I will not do something like that again, because it becomes such an ordeal and it isn't worth upsetting so many people (especially when it doesn't even actually work). However, when completely under the spell of my illness and in pure frustration with myself, at the time it always seemed like such an obvious and easy solution to escape from the constant white noise.

Chapter 23
VENTI SOYA FRAPPUCCINO LIGHT WITH SUGAR-FREE VANILLA SYRUP, DOUBLE BLENDED

Interlude, DIARY EXTRACT:

I am feeling crap, numb, alone, fat, lost, and these are only some of the adjectives I would use to describe myself right now.

I'm genuinely considering just quitting purging and letting myself get really huge. I feel as though I have so little self-respect, and pretty much no shame anymore, that there is no point in fighting against my natural fat and greed.

I binged all this weekend and I feel so fat and disgusting; but at the same time I just feel like eating more because my thin body is long gone now, and I don't seem to have any motivation or control to get it back.

I am hot and uncomfortable in this tight coat of skin that stretches across my fat and bloated stomach. I can feel the sheer volume of my bulging sides.

If I think about the scales I feel pure horror about my complete loss of inhibitions and caring. I'm trying to avoid thinking about them, as I am well aware of how much my weight will have shot up. I don't want to know or see the number; but avoiding it and pretending it does not exist only camouflages the problem, and I will carry on in this dreaded direction of fat and weight gain until I am morbidly obese. It's like when I've spent too much money and avoid checking my bank balance because I don't want to see it.

I am completely aware that I am trying to fill up a black hole inside me. Even just now I have bought another milky, sugary iced latte, even though I feel really sick and am already painfully full from today and the binging over the weekend. I feel completely helpless and as though I am always going to be using food like this.

My body disgusts me more than ever. I am neither happy nor content with the weight I am, or with the amount I eat. I can grab great handfuls of fat in my fists, everything about me looks fat, grotesque and wobbly. My body screams "NO SELF CONTROL", and "DISASTER" is written all over me in the form of red stretch marks and globules of cellulite. I am a failure, I have failed the people that I love, but more importantly I have failed myself.

By subconsciously punishing people through binges, I realise that it is me and me alone that suffers the consequences. I am the one rapidly gaining weight, feeling awful about myself and constantly being mentally and physically uncomfortable.

I can feel the amount of sweetener, soya milk and binge food that I consume, sloshing around in my stomach and intoxicating my body, causing it to swell. I know that to lose weight it will take time and that I need to stop binging and drinking. But I am really scared of failure. I've let myself go and used food as an easy option and comfort.

I desperately want to change and get back to being thin but I just don't know how anymore. I am lost.

Chapter 24
BAD TRIP

With any drug, after that first hit, you crave the same again, but it becomes more difficult to reach that same initial high. You search for something stronger, more intense, something that will be as good, or even better. As with any addiction, this spirals out of control so easily, leading you deeper and deeper into danger. Nothing will ever feel as good, nothing will get you exactly back there, nothing will be good enough or suffice, you will never reach that same euphoria, you will never be thin enough, so you keep going in your quest to recreate that indescribable same sensation you first experienced. It is a dark, dark pathway that leads you only into temptation, the power of the evil, forever and ever until death.

All the addictions I have experienced have a similar structure. Becoming a full time smoker – starting when drinking, then socially, then when bored, then in the morning, then twenty a day by accident. On to weed, a joint, two joints, every week, every night. Alcohol – one glass so easily turns to two, which in turn becomes a bottle, and then the next day, and the next day and every day. Anorexia – lose a pound or two, no, a stone, or two. But that is still not enough until you've lost five stone and are about to die, but even then you still don't think you look thin ENOUGH. You are never going to be able to achieve that initial high you so desperately want to feel again... Bulimia – one bite, the taste of the gods, one bowlful, two, three, four, you shovel it down your throat, food skimming across your taste buds, experiencing no flavour, trying to reach the non-existent point of satisfaction, until you have eaten so much that you just want to puke or die. Purging – just throw up once, no twice, just until you can see the tomatoes, no the pepper as well, may as well go for all of it, there is still more, keep going, you're not finished. There is always more.

When blinded by the trance of addiction, these behaviours become excruciatingly difficult to break and stop. You lose control before you can realise it, but once you realise, you feel like you are in so fucking deep that there is no way out. You are trapped in deadly cycles, and even though you know they are bad, they are there, and you cannot rub them out, only paint over them in the form of another addiction.

Walking down a short dark hallway (drunk and high) to the toilet, I suddenly have absolutely no idea who I am and I feel really sad and lonely. When I get into the light I look at my face in the mirror and do not recognise myself. The person staring back at me could be anyone, someone I have never seen or met before. I don't know what I want or who I am. Walking back down the dark hallway, the sudden wave of loss, insecurity and confusion hits me again. I am lost; I don't recognise anything. Someone bring me back, please. Help me.

And I feel sick. There is a tangled knot in my stomach; a combination of emotion and food, my abdomen is swollen with both. The sadness wells up inside of me and my eyes prick as they brim with tears of frustration, the realisation of the loss of my identity. I see this kitchen not as a place of family, feeding and nurture, but as cupboards packed with ingredients for recipes of disaster. The items stare me in the face, before leaping down my throat, brushing past my taste buds, then spreading evil across my body.

My stomach is like a cauldron, swilling and brimming with a mix of rancid food and toxic emotions, creating a strong potion of self hate.

Where the fuck am I? If I close my eyes will I wake up in the middle of the ocean? I have wandered miles now, searching for myself. Ambling down dark and twisted pathways in the cold silence, hoping that I may bump into myself and we will be able to reconnect, become one again. I will get to be myself again and finally remember who I was - who I am.

I can only remember sections of myself, things that upset me, things that made me laugh, things that I feared and things that I liked. But the cement that holds these bricks of memory together has worn away, disintegrated. Without this cement, the foundations of myself and the structure of who I am are lost, and I am just a pile of rubble. A mixture of emotions and memories scattered across the floor, some cracked, some strong, but missing the vital framework which seals them together.

Although several precious years of my life have been spent deep in the underworld, wasted away, I cannot regret my illness. Yes, it ruined a hell of a lot of aspects of my life, and had it not happened I might be a completely different person to who I am today. But the past cannot be changed. Maybe it happened as a valuable lesson to me, to appreciate life more, to be more grateful for what I have. Maybe it was supposed to happen so that in the future I will be able to help someone else, or so that I could write all of this. No one deserves the kind of hell an eating disorder drags you through. It has shaped my personality, given me a greater knowledge, understanding and sense of compassion though.

To everyone in my life that it has affected, I will always be truly sorry. I am also very sorry to myself for destroying a big part of me, which I'm not sure will want to return.

The feeling of falling, falling so fast, like when you suddenly jolt out of a dream, I will always remember very clearly. The starvation of the brain, the obsession, the adrenaline and that buzz and invincibility, but then the sudden dropping through the sky, no control, nothing to hold on to; it's the most frightening and crazy thing imaginable.

Chapter 25
A COME DOWN - 2013

2013 interlude:

'I am no longer completely suffocated by the illness, but our hands are still entwined, and the claws of Ana still dig sharply in to my fingers as we grip each other. She is still there, but at arms length now, no longer residing inside my body completely.

Anorexia is like an abusive lover; she harms you brutally, but you cannot help but return. It is so hard to completely let go of such a massive part of your life. The bruises and scars she has left on my body fade, but the ones in my mind don't. They remain as a reminder of a significant chapter of myself and are a story that will forever be etched into me.

I look at my body even today and I am so sure that I am not really here. My brain has a clear coating of Cling Film wrapped tightly around it. It acts as a barrier and prevents me from being "normal", and averts me from being able to fully connect with the world. I am still happiest when I am asleep, away from judgements, worries, thoughts, and reality. I escape to the purity of vivid and lucid dreams and away from the struggles and conformations of society. My dream world is my special place, where no one else can find me or see me and I cannot get hurt. I am taken so far away that I am removed from even myself and I love it.

Dream state is my favourite state and in some sense I believe I was trying to recreate this and bring it into my waking life when I was in a trance with my illness.

When actually awake, my eyes often haze over and I feel removed. I see something and it will take me a few minutes to register and process what it was and whether it was actually there or I imagined it. I walked around dazed, as if on clouds, sinking in and out of illusions with every footstep into the fluffy white nothingness. Things wash past me as I suddenly realise I am sinking through a cloud, so I quickly take a step and bring myself back to 'normality', or 'reality'.

The fact is, if you have anorexia, at some point you are going to have to recover - it is that, or die. Death is the easier option, sure, but going through recovery is the only thing that will give you life back. Determination is key and it is a fantastic trait that anorexics obtain. If you can starve to death, you can certainly eat to life. It's not fucking easy and it's ten times harder than actually getting ill was, in my opinion, but you CAN break away from the disorder and choose life when you realise that you really want to.

Like I have said, I still hold on to many aspects of my disorder, as it is still a recent and raw event in my life, but I am going in a better direction now than I was a year or so ago. One-step forward, three steps back is an extremely clichéd way to describe beating an eating disorder, but it is just that. Rather than being all consumed by the peculiar idea I had to starve myself, to be as thin as I could possibly be, I am now in two minds. I am split down the middle and have two halves of myself, one always holding on to an element of the illness, for example bulimia. The other half wants to live though, to get rid of all this hassle and heartache, all the sadness and pain. I don't want to worry about every morsel of food I put in my mouth and I want to be able to enjoy things without feeling the need to punish myself afterwards.

My choice of recovery came upon me when I decided that I was in fact, extremely thin, and maybe even thin enough. I was so sick in the body and the head that I literally couldn't do anything. I had proven to myself my immense perseverance and my ability to master an ultimate form of self control, which had subsequently forced everyone around me to notice me and take me seriously, whilst destroying both them and myself. When I lost everything I cared about though, I was left with nothing and felt truly alone. I was at my limit and had I gone an ounce further, I would be dead. Well done, I can be thin, I have control, I've had anorexia, I have nearly died, been there, done that, got the t-shirt, now fucking move on and get a life, is pretty much what I told myself. For the sake of my family, friends and my life, I had no option but to change pathways and step blindfolded into the confusing turmoil of recovering from anorexia, and start living.'

PART II

Chapter 26
CANDY FLOSS CRISIS

In the summer of 2014 I moved to Brighton with my best friend and it was a crazy, colourful mess. For months before, while I had been writing my book in Starbucks cafes all across London and she had been working on Oxford Street, we had been meeting for lunch every day and planning our move, our change. We both found jobs as soon as we had made the decision and sofa surfed until we found a house to move into with two other friends. I stayed in the kitchen of some friends of my brother and had an amazing time, continuing to write in the evenings. The decision to move out of my parents house was a massive step, as I had been recovering there for the past two years under their watchful eyes. I'd had all independence taken away from me, which is why moving out was the very first thing I desperately wanted to do as soon as I was strong enough. Although naturally my parents were worried as I was still suffering with quite severe bulimia, they couldn't stop me and supported me instead. Knowing that I would be living with my best friend Vicky, who had stuck by me throughout my illness, gave them some comfort.

I remember the night we moved to our new house on the seafront. It was a sunny day after work and I walked along the beach feeling so excited to see it. We bought some champagne and snacks to celebrate our achievement of making shit happen and ran up the steps to our new front door, super excited. My excitement combined with alcohol, slowly but surely changed to adrenalin and I found my legs marching me up to the local Tesco within half an hour of moving in, to purchase God knows what... boxes of cereal, soya milk, apple pies, crisps, cookies, cakes, anything made it into my basket. I remember feeling ashamed at the checkout, wondering if anyone knew what all the junk food I was purchasing was for, but that didn't stop me. I ran back to the house, shut myself in my new empty bedroom and ripped open the packaging in a frenzy, trying a bit of one thing then a bit of another, not even tasting what I was eating, just shovelling more and more down my throat. After what felt like hours of this, I finally came out of the episode and could barely move I was so full. Food was literally up to my throat as there was no more space inside my poor body. I knew immediately what was coming next, I had to purge. I didn't want to use the bathroom on the first night and didn't think it fair to Vicky, so instead, with tears of shame running down my face I climbed into my wardrobe with the Tesco bag, closed the door so it was pitch black and forced it all back up in darkness, shaking and weeping desperately sad tears.

The next day I woke up with an overwhelming feeling of shame. I was so disappointed in myself and couldn't believe that I had failed on my first night there. My stomach was horrendously bloated, eyes bloodshot, my head was aching and I was suffering terrible acid reflux as I dragged myself to work. I didn't know how I was going to be able to get through the day when all I wanted to do was kill myself. I did get through the day and I got very used to it because the above became an almost daily occurrence. I learned to endure the physical and mental pain that doing this every night caused me.

I would work all day in the vintage shop, alone, where I would have little to do but sit with my thoughts and feel horrendous about the previous night. The shop was on Sydney Street where I made many friends with the people in surrounding shops, and still to this day I'm sure they are unaware of how much their kindness helped me through some dark and difficult days. I enjoyed that aspect of work, the community, the friends I made on the street, the support people were giving me daily without realising... I just didn't enjoy being in isolation in the shop, and when it was quiet, it was so quiet.

There was a period of six weeks where two builders (Paul and Martin) were working in the shop everyday and if they ever happen to read this I want them to know how much they helped me and how much I appreciated their kindness. They listened to me, kept me company, helped me in the shop and we became good friends at the time. I missed them a lot once their work was finished, as for me, having them around made my days much brighter and my mind slightly less crazy.

As soon as I finished work I would race home, stopping at the wine shop on the way as I always felt as though a glass of Prosecco in the evening was such a lovely idea. Shame it never happened like that and one glass was impossible. A bottle or two would be consumed until I felt an episode coming on and would race to the shop to purchase a variety of binge foods, shut myself in my room, devour them, then make myself sick until the early hours; before going to work on three hours sleep, feeling horrendous yet again.

Although this was basically the routine I was still trapped in, Brighton gave me so much joy too and I will always think of it as my home. Vicky and I had countless hilarious nights out where were would drink in her room whilst getting ready and listening to Beyoncé. We would get dressed up, go out and go wild, drinking, smoking, meeting people and having fun. I have so many amazing memories of this period as although we both worked, afterwards, we were able to do whatever we wanted, whenever we wanted. Having that sense of freedom and independence back was indescribable. I finally felt my age again, which was one of the greatest rewards that choosing recovery had given me so far.

We would get very drunk, sit on the beach, watch the sea and walk home eating chips. Although this is standard behaviour for many people, for me the eating chips part always turned into a binge and once I arrived home, wasted, I would ruin my night by consuming everything and then having to purge once again for hours. The next day I would feel a combination of severely hungover and very, very sick. My swollen stomach was not only swimming with last night's alcohol, but also an awful combination of every type of food and acid. The shame I would feel when opening my eyes and seeing the mess of food wrappers, crumbs and sick around me was unbearable. I wished that I hadn't woken up to face what I had done and how I felt.

Often on days like these my dad would come to the rescue, get in his car and drive down to Brighton. We would go to Wagamama together, (my original 'safe food' place) and I would cry about what a disgrace I was as my dad would reassure me that it wasn't my fault and that I WOULD beat this. We would wander the lanes together, go somewhere to buy me some healthy food and he would then drop me back home once I was feeling a bit better.

215

Maybe I would last the night without binging, but maybe I would find myself walking up to the wine shop and the whole episode repeating itself once more. I was truly out of control of this thing inside of me and the vicious cycle I was trapped in seemed like it was inescapable. I started to believe that I would be stuck that way forever, as it was impossible for me to go more than one night without fucking up. It was as though the harder I tried the more I fell.

There were countless occasions where I would ring my parents on the walk home from work to ask for money for supper. I was lying. Or my eating disorder was lying. I threw all the money they transferred me away on binge food, feeling so wasteful as it all just went down the toilet, literally.

It was around this time that I started craving some kind of attention or affection, missing my ex and realising again what I had thrown away. I felt as though I had a massive void in my life which I was trying to fill with food through binging and I decided that this void was love (little did I know that the love I was seeking or missing, was love from myself). I believed that if I got a new boyfriend, my problems would somehow all disappear and I would want to look nice for them, so maybe I would stop binging and everything would go away. Deep down I knew this wasn't actually true, but I was a lost cause and looking for some kind of excitement, or thought that anything to fill my hollow self couldn't harm me more than I was already harming myself.

I joined 'Tinder' and started going on some meaningless dates which pretty much all either ended in disaster or amounted to nothing, which left me feeling rejected and even more empty than before. My binging and purging actually got worse because of this and although I didn't really care anymore and spent this time plastering over my feelings with alcohol, I was hurting deep inside.

I realised once again that my alcohol consumption was kind of a massive problem, but in comparison to the severe bulimia I was still suffering with, nothing really compared. I still knew that drinking was only making my episodes worse and more frequent, but I knew that regardless of the drink, I was still completely trapped in a binge purge cycle, drunk or sober. I tried everything, painting, writing again, cleaning my room, dying my hair all kinds of shades of bright pink, getting piercings, tattoos, plastering my face with dark makeup... literally anything to attempt to change myself and distract myself from those overwhelming urges, from what I was suffering, from what I was... but guess what, I couldn't escape myself, I couldn't change myself by altering the outside and over and over again I found myself slumped against the bathroom wall at three in the morning, covered in sick, knuckles bleeding and tears streaming down my makeup stained face.

My brother came to visit me one weekend and went with me to my first (and last) AA meeting. We walked to the church and were greeted warmly by all of the other alcoholics, offered tea or coffee and a chair. We sat in a giant circle and I just felt overwhelmed. The chanting of the rules and the introductions of 'hi my name is blah and I'm an alcoholic' was very scary.

I sat in the circle in silence and listened to the other alcoholics share their stories and explain their struggle with alcohol, intrigued as to why each and every one of them was there. I felt distraught. The Lydia I used to be at school, so good, pretty shy, very hard working... How did that young girl end up sitting in this circle.

They asked if anyone else wanted to say anything as the meeting was coming to a close. Somehow my shaking hand raised and my voice whispered with all the courage I had 'hi I'm Lydia and I'm an alcoholic. That's all I have to say'. Everyone replied in unison 'hi Lydia, thanks Lydia'. It was a truly mortifying experience and I ended up going home via the wine shop to repeat my usual cycle, feeling extra guilty about it for wasting my brother's time.

My life continued to unravel and tangle into a complete mess around me, if that was even possible. I was crying all the time as depression crept its way back to the centre of my life. It was at this point that I put my hands up in submission and really admitted I needed help once again. I physically could not live like this and I truly didn't want to.

I started taking prozac prescribed by my GP and although in a way this did help with my symptoms of depression, I also found it completely numbing. I was zoned out during the day, blank, slow... even if I felt more calm with my emotions, by the evening the same old habits would still manage to break through, which was so frustrating.

I started seeing a lovely therapist called Sarah once a week in the evenings after work. She practised cognitive behavioural therapy and was young and cool, which made a change from most of my previous therapists. She gave me worksheets to fill in about what I was eating, when I felt triggered, how to recognise different thinking patterns. I tried eating a grapefruit after every meal to use the sour taste as a signal I had finished eating. I tried lighting a candle during meal times and blowing it out once I was finished to signal the end of feeding. I tried making a box of things to go to, filled with old photographs, nail varnish, magazines, anything to do to distract myself if I felt an episode coming on. Although this was all helpful and actually even by just attending the appointments I was able to develop some kind of routine and new ideas, it didn't stop the bulimia and it was then that I truly began to actually accept that nothing ever would, that I was doomed to be this way for the rest of my life, fighting with food, hating my body, throwing up every day and suffering mental torture I inflicted upon myself.

Chapter 27
WHEN I SAW YOU RISE THE OTHER DAY I FELT MY WORRIES JUST SEEMED TO MELT AWAY INTO YOU

I continued attending therapy on a weekly basis and started focusing on other things, rather than desperately trying to fill the void. I started collecting old vinyl I found left around Brighton and decorating them. Quickly this became an obsession, but probably the healthiest one I'd ever had. As soon as I got home from work I would spend hours painting vinyl after vinyl with all different designs. Everyone seemed to love them so I set up a website to sell them. My room became covered in vinyl paintings and my head spilled with ideas of designs through my day at work. I actually began to look forward to getting home not to binge, but to paint.

During this time I also decided that I wanted to get a kitten. I thought that perhaps if I had to be responsible for taking care of someone else, it may force me to take care of myself too. This is when Mixie came into my life, a beautiful three month old kitten (from the woman at the wine shop, ironically).

I remember going to pick her up and feeling very scared about the decision I was about to make, but I did it anyway. I had always wanted a cat and believed that it was the right time and she could even help me.

I brought Mixie home in a box and really, she is one of the best things that ever came into my life. She was so tiny and I could see she needed me. I used to take her everywhere in her cat box (which she probably hated).

She stayed in my room with me and feeding her before myself sometimes helped me to slow down in making bad decisions. In spite of all the good things both painting and Mixie brought, you guessed it, I was still stuck. I remember feeling so guilty after an episode as she would be scared when she had to watch me binge. When I returned from purging she was always extremely calm, would come over and sit on my lap very quietly, as if she knew, which in turn would calm me, I wasn't alone. She knew I needed her. I remember when my brother came to visit and said, 'You've changed since you got Mixie', and I realised that he was right. I was somehow more calm.

I decided I was in love with someone who worked on the same street as me, a few shops down. I didn't know him well but he always smiled, said hello and offered to get me coffee. I pushed my thoughts to the back of my mind, knowing I would never have any chance with someone like that. No one would ever like me anyway, especially not if they knew the truth.

I asked Vicky one night whether I should just message him and ask him out for a drink or not... She said yes, so I did. I found this random wave of confidence and felt sick with anxiety as I typed the message, pausing for a long time with my finger over the send button before I just pushed it. I slammed my laptop shut and tried to forget I'd even sent it immediately, feeling so embarrassed by my decision. To my amazement, the same evening I got a response and it was a keen yes. I couldn't believe it and for some time really thought that he or his friends must be taking the piss out of me, or it must be a joke. Surely no one would ever be interested in me?

It wasn't a joke and from the Friday I went to meet him at the pub where we sat in the beer garden, we spent almost every day together for the next two and a half years.

Those first weeks of the new relationship saw me falling fast, experiencing pure joy like I couldn't even remember existed, feeling happiness, real excitement... and starting to let go of bulimia.

I went to my weekly therapy session a week or so after our first date and I just had nothing to say. My therapist couldn't understand how suddenly the miserable girl who sat crying and desperately trying to work out how to fix her life had just vanished. I was actually happy, I was buzzing and I couldn't believe how lucky I was. Suddenly the misery inside of me evaporated. My next session with

Sarah was the same, I had nothing to say at all, apart from that I didn't think I needed to come any more. That was our last session.

Our relationship developed at an extremely rapid pace. We saw each other every day because we only worked a few shops away. As I became more involved, I moved further and further away from my self-destruction, just naturally, without even trying.

I told him immediately about my struggles with anorexia, bulimia and mental health and he said he didn't care. I couldn't believe this was happening to me, it felt like some crazy dream beyond my imagination. I do remember him telling me that he didn't like it when I was sick. This worried me momentarily as it wasn't something I could control. But those words stayed in my head for the next three years and I stopped. Not just like that, but gradually I began to notice my binge / purge episodes were becoming less and less frequent. I never did it when he was around for fear of losing the relationship which really, I relied on extremely heavily.

I realised after a while that I hadn't taken my prozac... for weeks! I was so confused as to how I had just somehow forgotten to take the pill I relied on every single day to keep me sane and out of depression. I really couldn't believe it, it felt amazing.

Chapter 28
THE BUS TO YOKER

With my new relationship with my boyfriend developing and my old relationship with bulimia diminishing, I was feeling better and better every day. I felt like a new person and was completely amazed how the habits and issues I had dealt with for so many years, could just seem to melt away as someone walked into my life.

I decided to move to Glasgow with him; I had nothing to lose, only experiences to gain now I was finally getting on my feet for real this time.

I got a job within the first week in a high street clothing store, one I had wanted to work at for a long time. I was so happy and excited as everything seemed to be falling into place, just as I had wished.

The reality of the job wasn't quite what I had imagined and quickly I found myself becoming bored with retail, something I had never actually wanted to work in, but had just fallen into since my illness. Standing in the same spot all day folding clothes I couldn't afford, that customers unfolded over and over again, became tedious for me very rapidly and I found myself clock watching once more, counting down the minutes till my break, then the seconds until I could get back home. I didn't realise it at the time but I became extremely dependent on the relationship, which isn't really surprising since I had nothing or no one else up in Glasgow.

After six weeks of working and hating every minute of it (I didn't feel like I fitted in, or that I got to know anyone particularly well at all. I felt on edge and nervous much of the time, as well as bored), I got fired. I knew it was coming, as several days before when my parents came up to visit me, one manager said that I could leave early, before two others said I couldn't, just as I was about to go. The misunderstanding made it look like I was just leaving early because I wanted to, which wasn't actually the case, but they wouldn't listen. When I returned to work after a few precious days spent with my parents, I was asked to go to the manager's office. A large lump formed in my throat as I nervously walked to her door to be greeted by herself and another manager. They told me to sit down and asked me how I thought things were going, before explaining to me that they were letting me go. I couldn't believe it and stared at them in shock. When I asked why, they explained that I had been off too many times... this confused me as I had only been off sick twice, and both times were genuine. They also said that it seemed as though I 'was only there for the money', to which I thought, isn't everyone? They told me I had a week's notice, so back to the shop floor I went where I stood frozen in one spot holding back tears as I tried to continue with my shift knowing that I'd just been fired. I didn't understand that I could just leave, until one of them saw how upset I was and told me that I could. Within seconds, tears were streaming down my face. I ran to the staffroom, grabbed my stuff and never went back. I felt so unbelievably shit, worthless and embarrassed. I had never, ever been fired before and couldn't quite believe I'd got fired from something I found so uninspiring, so basic, so easy. It was possibly one of the biggest confidence-crushers I had ever experienced, especially after feeling like I had come so far.

I spent the whole bus journey home crying tears of shame, wondering what I was going to say, how I was going to explain that I had lost my job, wondering what to do now. The sympathetic response I was so accustomed to from the years of my family and friends learning to understand me and make exceptions for me, wasn't there. I was so confused as I wasn't used to having to deal with things independently, I was used to having people to lean on, people to tell me it wasn't my fault, that it was fine, they'd help me find something better. This different reaction in most circumstances would be normal, frustration, worry, maybe disappointment... But to me I felt let down by it, I guess because it wasn't what I was used to and it was hard for me accept.

I spent the next months or so in the house on the computer searching for jobs, all day, every day. I felt utterly useless, pointless, bored, alone and isolated. No matter how many things I applied for, I wasn't hearing anything back. I spent endless days walking round and round Glasgow in the pouring rain handing CV's into every single shop, only to hear nothing. I started to become depressed again and found I was eating more because I had little else to do. The weight I was gaining was making me as miserable as my unemployment was.

Eventually I found a Christmas temp job at Waitrose on Byers Road and thankfully passed the interview process. I started work on the first of December. From day one I was completely motivated as I was desperate to not have a repeat of my previous experience. I worked as hard as I could and as many hours as they would give me up until Christmas, and started to feel better again.

Christmas was spent in Glasgow, my first ever one away from home. New year was spent away and was really fun too, however I knew that when I came back I would have no job again. I signed on to job seekers allowance and the next couple of months were spent in the same way as the previous few, looking for jobs, feeling useless and struggling with boredom and loneliness in the house by myself.

My desperation to find work, or at least anything to do with myself during this time of unemployment, led me to sign up for a Beauty Therapy course with a charity called the Princes Trust, and I got a place. The course was six weeks long and a bit like going to school again. Finally I met some people which really helped me, as did learning something new. Whether or not I actually wanted to develop a career within that field was kind of besides the point. The fact that I was getting out of the house every day, using my brain and being sociable was more important and more helpful to me than anything else I had done since moving there.

During the course, I continued to sign on at the job centre and found out that a new Waitrose was opening in Milngavie. Because I had been a Christmas temp, my chances of getting the job were greatly improved, so I applied and I got it! The store was due to open a week after my course ended, which was perfect timing and I finally felt like I was getting somewhere. My first book 'Raw, The diary of an Anorexic', was also published and released around this time, which was really exciting for me and I spent a couple of weeks being interviewed and doing some publicity for it.

I started at Waitrose in May and although the journey was a little awkward to get there everyday, I put all my effort and energy into that job, working hard and making friends. The people I met there were so kind and it was really special for me to feel part of something there in

Glasgow, as up until that point I had felt very alone and struggled a lot to find my place.

Chapter 29
HEARTBREAK, SOBRIETY-BREAK

After spending a year and a half in Glasgow, my boyfriend and I went travelling in Thailand for three months, before moving back to the South of England. I moved back into my parents house as I had spent all my money travelling; he found his own flat.

In January I had my heart broken.

As I got used to the centre of my life missing and the pain of loneliness at night, I began to let myself develop my own personality, become myself, my true self. I became more open to talking to new people and let my sense of humour shine through. Slowly I began to crawl out of the shell of protection I had built around myself years ago without even realising. My personality changed from a wilted autumn leaf - quiet, reserved, breakable, to a strong, bright flower, alive, colourful and noticeable. I let other people in and I let myself out, which I hadn't truly done since my first year of University. I realised in many ways I had continued to isolate myself through the relationship, and a lot of my happiness depended on that alone.

After three months smoke free, I decided to start again. After almost two years alcohol free, I decided to start again. After almost three years of excluding myself from most social situations, I decided to start again. I decided to say yes to everything, after saying no for so long. I decided to try everything, to not give a fuck because I had nothing to give a fuck about anymore. This quickly turned into an escapade of 'YES'S' and a continuous time of questionable decisions, most of which were influenced by alcohol.

My re-found habits of smoking and drinking started small and tame, social, harmless. Very quickly, without even realising, both habits became full on addictions once more. Before I knew it I was inhaling 20 cigarettes a day again and drinking every single night, sometimes during the day too. At first it was all fun and games, it was because I fucking deserved to 'have fun', I had earned it. I was staying out late, not letting my body get any rest and just not taking care of myself. My stomach was sore and bloated the majority of the time and I reached a point where the depression and shame of the alcohol from the night before, combined with a daily hangover was becoming too much. I wasn't having fun anymore, I didn't feel good.

The break up itself was erased from my mind within a couple of weeks of it happening. I never moped around looking through old photographs or listening to songs that reminded me of the good times, or the bad times. Perhaps I'd had enough depression that my head simply said no more, no more sadness, no more crying, you've had enough.

I plastered over everything with alcohol-infused nights and partying. I surrounded myself with alcohol and other people who would drink it with me every night. I created endless memories and built friendships that are very strong, however for me I realised that this environment was toxic for my mental health, that I couldn't handle it like everyone else, that I was becoming both dependent and depressed.

My weight began creeping back up due to the alcohol consumption and increase in appetite, largely due to hangovers. I felt very unhappy with my body once more and was constantly bloated, tired, felt horrendous about myself and didn't like who I was becoming. I relapsed a couple of times after returning home at 3 in the morning after working all day and drinking all evening. Binging and purging never felt so bad and I didn't even have the energy for that shit like I used to. More often than not I would end up passing out in my room only to be rudely awakened by my brain-piercing alarm just several hours later to repeat the whole process.

I started feeling like the drinking was affecting me negatively, that my three month long stomach ache and weight gain might be a symptom of alcohol abuse. I was becoming tired and realised that I wasn't just drinking for my own entertainment anymore, I was drinking because it was a habit that had very quickly become so ingrained in me again.

Chapter 30
CHAMPAGNE YOGA

During the next couple of weeks I was truly desperate to stop drinking, managing a few days without, before crashing back down. I took up yoga, as I thought one of the best ways to give something up is to replace it with something positive. I figured if I had to wake up at 6am to do yoga before work, there was no way I'd be able to drink the night before. My mum had been telling me for the past however many years that I should practise yoga and I had ignored her. I decided maybe, just maybe she had been right all along and this was the answer I had been looking for.

I felt like a chaotic contradiction going to yoga at 6am one day, starting to let go, feeling positive and alive because of it, then drinking and smoking twelve hours later when it got dark, and waking up feeling that sinking feeling once more. I felt shit doing this, I felt stupid and it felt pointless, but I knew that it wasn't pointless, so although people may have wondered what I was trying to do here, how contradictory my behaviours were, I didn't give up. As I continued to attend classes, slowly the benefits of yoga started to outweigh the temptations of alcohol. I realised the peacefulness I felt as I walked out of the studio after class was becoming more important and more enjoyable than giving into alcohol cravings and the fake high that created. During the relaxation at the end of my first class, I found myself feeling extremely emotional. It was the fact that I had plucked up the courage to attend the class alone, decided to do something purely for myself that was actually beneficial to my health, made a decision to commit to something new, and felt more relaxed than I had ever felt.

I became completely absorbed in my new love of yoga, attending classes up to four times a week and practising in my bedroom every single night. As well as benefiting my physical health through movement and stretching my body, the mental side of the practice worked wonders for my anxiety and helped me to let go of negative thoughts I still had towards myself.

I became inspired to master the press handstand, which I have worked on every single day since. Having a goal based on strength, balance, patience and practise was almost life changing for me. When upside down, I realised that I had no option but to be totally present in the moment, as all my concentration was required; there is no space for thoughts, just beautiful, quiet stillness.

As I have continued to practise daily and watched myself improve, I have felt proud of myself for putting in the work, persevering and not giving up. Handstands have allowed me to develop a focus I didnt realise I had, made me feel more calm than anything else and have enabled me to become a more positive person than I ever have been, which in turn makes me more pleasurable to be around. Finding a way to nurture my own mind first, allows me to give more joy and light to other people, and I've noticed a huge difference in my relationships with others since incorporating this daily practice into my life.

Chapter 31
A PERSONAL RETREAT

I spent the month of December avoiding alcohol, trying to change my diet to get rid of the bloating and trying to clear my mind as best I could. I booked tickets to Australia and Bali to go away for a month by myself, to reflect, to find some peace and to take a step back from everything that had been going on around me.

This journey has taken all the self confidence I was able to muster and it hasn't been easy. But right now I am thirteen hours into my first flight, completely alone and I am smiling. I don't feel anxious, bored, scared or alone. I feel ready, strong, decisive, calm and happy. The fear of the unknown does not feel like a fear, it feels like an opportunity to better myself as much as possible in the space of these thirty days which I give to myself as a gift. I don't want to waste a second of this precious time I may not get again for a long time, which is why I am in the sky right now, already writing, already breathing, already practising mindfulness and cutting myself off from the world below me, the small world I had been sucked into, that I let affect me, hurt me, change me.

I am leaving behind yet another chaotic chapter and I am glad about it. I will miss my family so much and my friends who are my family too, however everything became too complicated for my brain to cope with. I'm removed and I am fucking happy about it. I have made the decision to press pause on everything else to allow myself time to heal, time to grow.

I want to see how much I can learn about myself in this month, without alcohol, with exercise and mental clarity, building healthy habits and practising stillness.

Interlude: I've touched down in St Kilda and the atmosphere that I have been welcomed to has been exactly what I have been trying to escape. It is day one and I spent the day wandering alone, trying to be content with myself, facing my fears of eating alone in restaurants, facing myself and containing my anxieties about what I am doing. On returning home (the home in which I will be staying) I am faced with offers of alcohol, which I graciously accept in order to look open and accepting of others' lifestyles and cultures while I stay in their place. Two drinks in and the atmosphere becomes chaotic for me, chaotic like in London. People spilling their drama and painful life experiences to me like I am some kind of therapist, but I feel like a sponge. As I absorb the turbulence of pain in their lives and the unrequested advice and messages they throw at me, I feel like a mess again, I feel disrupted, interfering energies, pushed off balance. How come that even though I am on the other side of the world, in the first

24 hours the very things I am trying to take myself away from, have followed me here, and I ask myself why. Why can I not find peace. I feel unsettled now, which means that I am going to have to work extra hard to focus on my goals and what I am here to achieve. I will not waste these days using alcohol and remaining in the same place, or going backwards even. I will not let people suck me in. I will be alone, I will focus on what I must achieve in these twenty nine days, and I will fully trust myself that I am the only person who can give myself advice, that the things I know about myself already are the things that will get me closer to where I want to be.

I cast my mind back over the past 26 years and look for a time since I came into the world, when I let myself be completely alone, undisturbed by the people or situations around me, silent and letting myself be with myself, letting myself breathe, giving my brain a break... that time doesn't exist. There is not one moment in my entire life since I was born that I've disconnected myself from the build up around me, the spinning wheel of life gathering more and more atoms in the form of characters, influencers, substances, situations, emotions, relationships until I've become spider-webbed by life.

Right now I am trying to break apart that web, cut each thread away with my mind by letting things go, finding the things I need from within, rather than through anything or anyone else.

I decided that last night's chaos and the place I've ended up staying is yet another test; life likes to test me - it makes me stronger. This could be life's way of letting me know that I cannot run away from my problems, no matter where I go they will always follow me, until I finally understand and acknowledge that I need to change the root of the issues - myself. You can change your location as much as you like, you can change the people around you as much as you like, but in the end it is what's inside yourself that you need to understand and learn to be content with and grateful for in order to find true happiness.

Chapter 32
A PROPHET

I woke up this morning after a deep sleep feeling more clear of my goals than ever. I didn't feel bad about yesterday, I didn't feel guilty, low, nor numb. I felt ready.

At 6am I left the house. I could still hear the jargon-chatter from the room next door as the characters who erupted into my life last night continued their chaos. Rather than let those sounds make me feel anything, I chose not to hear them, not to listen, to remove myself, to do my own thing.

I went to find the yoga studio close to the house, but it was closed, so instead I took myself running along the seashore. The silence of the beach in the morning made me feel calm, peaceful. I passed the pier and spotted a man at the very end, dressed in all white, sitting cross legged, meditating. I looked at him and felt inspired by what he was doing, connected somehow. On my way back, he was still there, practising Tai chi. I decided to stop, to sit, to watch this still moment in time. After a while, he began to walk along the pier towards the beach, towards me. As he approached, still making motions and gestures with his arms, we made eye contact. I held my gaze for a few moments and then smiled. He smiled back and continued to practise, right in front of me. I couldn't understand his broken English too well as he began to speak, but he got me standing up, opening my arms to the sea and looking to the sky before bringing my hands back to prayer and repeating over and over again, side by side in silence on the empty beach. When he stopped, I stopped. He began to speak once more and told me that I need to stop drinking, to stop smoking, that we need to give in order to make space to receive love, and love is all I need. I looked at him in amazement wondering how he was able to know such deep things about me within moments of us meeting; it was crazy. He asked why I was here on the beach in Melbourne. I explained to him that I was trying to stop drinking, to stop smoking, to find peace with myself, to better my life, to practise yoga and mindfulness and to eventually achieve self-love. He nodded as I spoke. He asked if he could say a mantra for me. "When?", I asked. "Now," he replied. "Come. it will take five minutes of your time". I looked at the time and even though I should be getting back in time for yoga, I agreed to stay. Maybe yoga had found me.

I followed Pueblo down the pier to the end and he told me to sit on one side while he sat opposite at the other. Cross-legged and eyes closed he told me to breathe. As I breathed in the fresh sea air he started chanting, long, slow, beautiful sounds. Apart from his voice the only thing I could hear was the sound of the gentle waves breathing in and out against the shore.

It suddenly became warmer and as I opened my eyes again the sun was emerging from behind the clouds, drenching the glowing beach with its warm light. Pueblo was smiling as I pointed out the sunlight. We bowed to each other and then came to our feet to walk back down the pier. We spoke a little more in Spanish, I told him about where I work and he told me where he was from. He shook my hand several times looking me straight in the eye and into my soul, with a smile on his face that spoke to me without words. As he disappeared into the distance, I looked around, wondering if I had imagined what had just happened. It was so surreal and I wasn't sure if Pueblo was real or was my subconscious' way of sending me an important message. He was real, but I also believe I needed to see him and he gave me something I won't forget, ever. I never saw him again.

Chapter 33
CONCLUSION

I've been so lost for so many years. I look back at the journey I've been on up until now and am bewildered as to how I found my way through all the obsessions, addictions, mental turmoil, situations, pain, chaos and traps. I feel unbelievably proud to be able to say that I finally found my way back to myself, however long it took me.

Eating disorders are still widely misunderstood. Continuing to raise awareness and share stories of hope and recovery is one way I am able to attempt to better people's understanding of the mind of the sufferer. It may also be useful in distinguishing patterns as to how the illness develops and manifests itself in someone.

My recovery story is not perfect - it is far from it, but that is why I wanted to share it. As you have read, I relapsed occasionally, I went up and down, falling back into the traps of addiction and dependency on unhealthy habits over and over again. But recovery usually isn't one smooth path and I wanted to show you that. Time and perseverance though, can and will heal you, if you let it. The strongest thing you can do is to keep standing back up when you fall, as many times as it takes. Relapses don't make you weak, they make you strong.

I've learned so many things through this experience and the most important lesson and achievement of them all, is that I am able to be totally self-sufficient, able to feel happiness without relying on anyone or anything else to give it to me. I am able to feel content with who I am, alone.

Every negative has been a positive in that it has taught me an important lesson. Every person who has hurt me, disappointed me, let me down or used me, has given me something invaluable which I am so grateful for and have been able to use to reach where I am right now. Every person who has stood by me, listened to me and supported me, has taught me love, real love that I will always be so grateful for. I wouldn't have been able to get here without that. Each hurdle that has blocked my path, has forced me to summon some inner energy to leap, climb or crawl over it, showing me that with my own strength and determination, I am able to overcome anything. Every battle I've fought with the voice in my head, has led me to realise how powerful the mind is. Every piece of useless advice given to me has demonstrated that my own advice to myself is the most valuable, because no one knows me like I know me, no one has had the lessons I've had, they have had different ones significant to themselves and their lives. The journey I've been on with myself has been so turbulent, but in the end it has brought me closer to myself; I am able to understand my own complicated mind.

I firmly believe that full recovery from both anorexia and bulimia is possible. When people told me that full recovery was unlikely or that some symptoms of your eating disorders will always remain with you throughout your life, I chose not to believe them and I chose well. I am one of many who are living proof that recovery is one hundred percent possible and you are not doomed to a life of disordered eating after being affected by an eating disorder. Sure, you may have painful memories of your experience and that chapter of your life might never be easy to reflect on, be open about, or be forgotten, but what you will have is an outlook on life that you can eventually use to your benefit and a knowledge of yourself that will be so deep because of the journey you've been on. You will be more compassionate towards others because you will understand in great depth the true meaning of mental pain. You will be mentally strong because you've fought and won a battle that one time you probably thought was impossible; maybe everyone else thought it impossible too. You will be living proof that the impossible is possible, and that is something truly special.

When you make that last step and decide to completely let go of your eating disorders make believe hand, you will finally be alone, free to live. That freedom is the key to happiness. Letting go completely may be scary at first, it took me a very long time as subconsciously I didn't want to move forward without some aspect of the disorder remaining with me, it was my identity. But once you get that first taste of freedom, once you are able to rid yourself of the ashes of Ana, realise you don't fucking need that, you will feel so damn liberated and you will know you deserve it. Something my yoga teacher has been repeating every day is that 'when you let go, you create space to receive'. Leaving things behind you and truly letting go of the negativity in your life really does create space for good things to enter. Recently yoga and meditation have become an important part of my life and I find the physical and mental benefits incredible. I only wish I had listened to my Mum all those years ago when she tried to persuade me to take it up then, when I was in the midst of the turbulent recovery process. I truly believe it is a practise that would have helped and benefitted me so much then, if it can help me this much now. I would highly recommend it to anyone in recovery or suffering with a mental health illness.

Recovery is different for every individual. What works for one person might not work for you. Be patient. Trial and error is key. Explore every option and be open minded in trying new things. Forgive yourself when you slip, it is natural, it is a lesson, it is there to teach you how to do better, how to overcome obstacles. For me, the conventional forms of recovery such as hospitalisation, day-care , dieticians, psychiatrists, weighing and counting, didn't work. I do however know many other people who have recovered successfully that way and probably more quickly than me. I was unable to connect with any of those treatment plans and found my path through cognitive behavioural therapy, mindfulness, my family and friends, love, travel - seeing new and exciting things showed me that there was so much more to life outside of my illness. Tasting independence once I was well enough made me hungry for more. I know many people who have discovered a love of yoga or fitness which has helped them combat their eating disorders and turn their unhealthy obsessions into healthy ones. I know people who have used art therapy, studying or volunteering to recover. Writing also always helped me a lot as letting everything out onto a blank piece of paper made my head feel less heavy. There are so many options, so don't give up if something isn't working for you or helping you, you may need to give it time, or you may need to move on to the next thing. Try everything and don't give up.

To the families and friends of those suffering, your unconditional love and support is one of the most important aspects of your loved one's recovery. Although they may not know or show how much it means to them, no matter how frustrating and heartbreaking this illness is to watch, keep loving them, keep lifting them, keep encouraging them to get better. It will be so hard at times, as you may feel as though you aren't talking to your loved one; they are hidden, buried and crushed beneath the mental illness which can be so deceptive, cruel and manipulative. Your understanding is so important and although it is incredibly difficult for you to watch, try your best to educate yourself on eating disorders and provide the best kind of support you can.

I feel so happy right now, lying in a hotel room on the other side of the world, completely alone. How peaceful it is to not have anyone with me, including a mental illness. How relaxing it is to not have to battle a voice in my head for every waking moment. Loneliness and boredom were always two of my main triggers and I never thought the situation I am in right now could be possible, without chaotic disasters of self-sabotage occurring. But here I am, fully recovered, happy, truly content with my body for the first time ever in my life and so excited about the next chapters that I will be able to create and enjoy, free from my past, free from eating disorders.

It has taken me until now to realise that the void I was constantly trying to fill with something, that thing that I always felt was missing inside me, was self-love. Searching and attempting to fill it with such negative things for so long without realising that I was the only one who could fill it - by loving myself first. The answer was within me all along. I am amazed by the challenges I have faced and the lessons I have been taught along the way to the realisation that the most important thing I have ever learned, was perhaps the most simple. I am finally able to love myself and truly appreciate that accepting myself for who I am, is the only way to let go, to create that space to move forward from my eating disorders and welcome other, new, exciting and meaningful things into my life.

I am enough.

Printed in Great Britain
by Amazon